Kind Growth

A
FES Life!

Author: Kim Green

Editor: Angela Adkins
Cover Art: Zeke Anderson
A2Z Designs

Special thanks to Jan Brandvik and Ingrid Brandvik for responding to my banter and helping me navigate ways to write about sensitive subjects.

Additional thanks and hugs to Brooklyn Green for sitting at the computer helping me hour after hour! I wrote this book to leave a legacy and having you participate in that legacy is incredibly special to me.

Table of Contents

KIND GROWTH

The FES (Foreign Exchange Student) Life!

"It takes the largest amount of courage to be kind and the smallest amount of wisdom for growth." - Kim Green

When you make your hypothesis and predict your outcome, the process of kindness and growth is simple. The reality of kindness is - that it sucks! It drags you into emotions, presents opportunities for failure, and challenges the things you believed as truths.

True growth is equivalent to broken bones, pulled muscles, and torn ligaments. Growth isn't a fluid motion that just

7

happens; it's what happens after the pain. So why do it? Why take on an international student and be kind? Why ask your family and friends to endure the growth with you? It's a simple process and it's called acceptance. The challenge is, can you really accept someone? Different is Different, Different is NOT necessarily Wrong.

Acceptance through personal growth is incredibly confusing. You know life around you. You understand the merry-go-round procedures and can behave accordingly to what is your culture. You do not question if what you know is right or wrong; you just accept it as normal. Normal looks different all over the world. I would never advocate for someone from the USA to think the same as someone from Ethiopia but appreciating our differences is vital. If you're proud of your culture, never be ashamed of it. Embrace it. It created the space where you grew.

At the same time, don't back away from the challenge of change. We all have miraculous parts of our cultures and we all have dark spots too. Identifying those differences for the means of equality is a kindness we all need to demonstrate. In the same fashion, do not change your culture by abdicating the history of it. Whatever history you have, evaluate it. Are you offended by it? Are others offended by it? Good! Strive to grow from it, don't erase it like it didn't happen. Learn from it, accept it, do better than rising in anger to promote change, be the change you want the world to see. You, yourself, make the sacrifice, and, as in my case, be willing to commit to kind growth even when it's hard!

A quick internet search in 2008 led me to this brilliant idea of hosting a FES (foreign exchange student – thank you creds to that 70's show). It's a perfect plan of blending culture, an opportunity to bring diversity to my small hometown. It's a way to show my kids the world and teach them differences. It's culture, diversity, and it's brilliant! A little additional research showed we have to do some background checks, a home inspection (I better clean under the stove!), a few classes, show finances, then provide a room, bed, food, and a place to study for the FES. Beginning the process of hosting is a lot like getting recruited for college sports.   In college sports, coaches and schools alike roll out the red carpet, give away free t-shirts, plan lunches with staff and administration, and an abundance of creative compliments crafted specifically to draw the student into their school and program. Then once the student is committed, he arrives at campus, gets shoved in a block dorm, juggles class schedules, barely survives the physical aspects of practice, let alone the beat down from the coach and others critiquing his performance.

Hosting FES organizations parallel that behavior by telling you every magical thing about having an international child. They make it sound like it will be a walk in the park on a sunny day. Organizations present these kids as the best, and in some ways they are. Then you arrive at the airport to pick up your FES and the truth is it's another teenager living in your home and most walks are not so sunny! Like life, if you're going to find the rainbow, you're probably going to have to play in the rain.

A few phone calls later we have checked all the boxes (I FORGOT TO CLEAN UNDER THE STOVE) and we get to pick our new family member. The agencies give you letters from the student (and I guarantee most kids have their parents write it). You're given some interests, hobbies, grades, and health histories of the kids. There is a fact or collection of interests on each profile that ultimately appeals to you and while some are profound, others, like our first FES, are simply a couple facts about what he likes. The facts on our first FES said he liked video games and sports. Yep, as shallow and simple as that! As a family we selected him because of video games and sports. Honestly, we had no idea what type of kid would blend with our family. Our kids liked sports and games, so it seemed logical enough to go with those interests.

Here is where you really need dramatic music to set the scene for this perfect situation. Here we are, being so kind to this poor unfortunate kid from another country whose life is so void his only dream is to spend a year in America. Who by profile wastes his life away on video games? This kid who we plan to embrace and make him a member of our family because obviously his home life is less than. We will introduce him to new foods, show him our beautiful country, and share our ways! We will teach our religion and show him God every Sunday, ok, maybe only 2x a month, possibly COE (Christmas and Easter only) attendance, oh screw it, we might honestly never go, but don't judge! Aren't we simply the most generous family you could ever meet?   Isn't it quite possible we will sprout angel wings any moment? If I had a nickel for every time someone shared an accolade with me in regards to hosting I could probably buy an incredible pair of new boots (I am a realist, it probably wouldn't make me rich).

So, we did it. We jumped into the world of international living and loving. We were kind and it sucked! We grew and it hurt! My family discovered so many pieces of life that have absolutely nothing to do with culture and everything to do with acceptance. Each of us embraced the good and the bad that came with identifying our own flaws and shortcomings. No matter the situation, the country, the personalities, we became a family with these kids (and their natural families) all around the world. Our very first international family dug in deep and haven't let us go yet…and that is why we continued for over a decade to embrace all the wonderful differences in our world and how we painfully came to appreciate the freedom of acceptance.

Chapter 1

Norway

2008

The call came on a Thursday afternoon, the life changing phone call – it's all approved! The boy we picked is ours! We received the flight information and just like that we had another child! On Sunday! Sometimes the exchange process organically moves that fast. We made a decision and about sixty-five hours later we were headed to the airport. It's important if you decide to host (which I hope some of you consider) to be comfortable with the word NO.

I was nowhere ready for my first international son. It showed many times through his year here. It showed in my thought processes! I actually thought to myself, "We are for sure going to make his life so much better than he could ever imagine." We live in America, right? It is the greatest country ever and all that. Our family found ourselves at the airport, with signs, balloons, and matching shirts. Everything we planned was to welcome this boy home to our life as a family. We had discussed how we must be careful with this poor creature because he's just left his home, his family, and everything he knows. We thought we understood the language barriers and tried to pre-plan every situation to make him comfortable. We even let people know we weren't taking visitors for a few days so our fragile new son could acclimate! We had no expectations except to be the best host family we could be. The excitement of knowing how much we have to share with him is overflowing in each of us.

Finally, he's there…. walking through the gate! It is that moment we expected and waited for. We adored him instantly and the hugs were exact perfection. Introductions made and we are impressed he actually identified everyone and his pronunciations were on point. We repeatedly tried to pronounce his name correctly - but I beg you - when you host a FES just give up on the name pronunciation! Lazy American tongues just don't sound the same. Besides, every FES I have ever met comes to appreciate the "nickname" I creatively make with my inability to correctly pronounce their actual names! Moving on, and because we are so kind, we help him get his luggage and head toward the car.   Could this be any better? We asked some questions back and forth and this first meeting was rather awkward, but we chose to venture on. For some reason I asked the question, "What do you think of Americans?"

His answer literally changed my life! This poor creature, far from home, fulfilling his dream of a year in America, who I had built in my head as this person whom I was going to change his life and make so much better - turned the tables completely within 10 minutes of meeting him with his answer. He kind of smirked at me, and said "you want honesty"? Did I? Sure I did...hit me with it! He responded: "Americans are fat and lazy."

"Americans are fat and lazy." It echoed as he said it.

I mean what? who? Did he really just say that? He sure did, and it was the most honest and pure answer. It was different than anything expected. Pause for a piece of wisdom I learned: The word "expected" should never apply to the process of hosting FES because expectations are only going to lead to failure. Back to the story, thoughts were flying through my mind as I processed his view of

15

Americans. I mean, just because I stay on the positive side of the scale doesn't mean I am fat and lazy......does it? Why exactly did he want to come to America if Americans are fat and lazy? What did he think he would gain from spending a year with fat and lazy people? More importantly, did *I* think Americans were fat and lazy? Profound moments like that often take a bit to sink in, and this one took a while to sink all the way in.

It took a long while. It has been over a decade of living the FES life and it's still an ongoing process. My goal in writing my journey is 1) to entertain you with some interesting situations. 2) to support exchange organizations because they are so dear to me and my growth. I certainly want to leave a tangible tale for all my kids, biological and international, so they know I tried to live a purposeful life. 3) to multiply what I have learned. I want my kids to know I realized how fat and lazy I was and I did something about it. I found truth in this process and it presented an opportunity to better myself. I want you to join in the self-discovery process of hosting a FES student. Don't ever blame anyone for your station in life. If you want to grow - you can - and I promise it will hurt like hell! Grow anyway! Don't side step confrontational topics, explore them, and take on the challenge of being an FES host family.

back to my FES story…

We arrived home and I was all excited to help him unpack and settle in, he on the other hand had checked and knew the Minnesota Twins would be playing, so he literally jumped over the back of the couch and assumed the baseball watching position. Suitcases sat there mocking me as their owner watched baseball. I tried a few times to start conversations and learned he was particularly singular in his focus where Twins baseball is concerned. My husband seemed to think this was a great option for the evening's activity and actively encouraged eating pizza in the living room! I decided when you can't beat them, join them instead, and look forward to a different scenario for tomorrow.

Tomorrow came and his room was messy, he took FOREVER in the shower, he couldn't keep a schedule (unless it's the Twins), he ate more food than normal, he was a little cocky, and he left the toothpaste lid off! He's not even a true exchange student; I discovered he had dual citizenship! He and our oldest son can't stand each other - I was pretty certain that bloodshed was in the near future. He came and went and some of his new friends made me anxious. He consistently left his cup on the counter, he didn't rinse his plate, and he kept forgetting to tell me thank you for all these kind opportunities I have paved the way for

17

him to enjoy! I had to remind him to take the trash out and make curfew! He rolled his eyes every time someone asks if he has a taco bell in Norway. A week in and guess what…. HE IS 100% A TEENAGER! And the sad thing is it wasn't him with the problem, it was me. I read the material handed to me and drank the Kool aid! I saw rainbows and butterflies when he saw a plane ticket to America for 10 months away from family to do whatever he wanted to do!

That was my first lesson in how lazy American's can be. How lazy I was. I took the 10 page pamphlet and thought I understood the culture of another country. I read things like cultural dishes of fisheye pudding, vikings, no sunlight/constant rain and figured, "No wonder he wants to come here." I didn't bother to research actual current data or specifics on his country. I just accepted some papers handed to me, did what I thought was my due diligence, and moved on.   That was a lazy exploration of someone's home country.

As a future potential host family, I advise you - DO NOT read the pamphlet of information on another country. ASK your potential FES or ask his family. Each town, city, or territory varies tremendously - just like here in the USA! One pamphlet does not teach about an entire country. Assumptions about culture simply based on a location isn't acceptance or understanding of a culture. Assumptions are lazy ways of being unwilling to learn.

Our oldest child at the time was 14 and our FES was 17 so as parents we had not yet dove into the waters of high school. We got a crash course with our FES! Learning how much I hovered was another hard acceptance. Lazy.... too lazy to teach my kids and trust them to follow those lessons. I preferred to shelter them from information and protect them from harm. If I am not going to teach them about life, how can I expect them to make decisions in life? By not teaching them, I retained control because they needed me for answers. Being needed felt good, but wasn't necessarily good for them. Learning life lessons from a 17 year old FES.... darn it! This boy who had parents that felt he was mature enough to cross the pond and stay an entire year with strangers. I wanted an 11pm curfew. Can I hear a bad "Helicopter parent" shout out!

Through this revelation I was having, I began systematically letting go of issues I controlled. Eating all your vegetables, morning showers, curfews, friends, doctors, tests, and so much more. What I learned was the more opportunities I allowed for my children to make positive choices, the more good decisions were made. Now wait - they are still kids and they still made some questionable choices, but the point was they had to own the results both good and bad.   Fast forward and as a parent I really have no rules now. Instead, I have conversations that circle around facts and consequences, but I allow my kids to decide. My kids often say I "Mind Fuck" them (their words not mine) but really I just make them accountable to their choice, and I suppose that can feel the same. I can't control their storms, but I can teach them ways to react, and adjust their sails. Allowing them to be hurt and feel hurt isn't fun, but their social emotional growth is worth my discomfort. I no longer hover over their decisions, I just wait to see if their decision is positive or if I need to step in. Helicopter mama has turned into more of an Apache helicopter - on standby if needed.

Our oldest son, and our first FES settled into a territorial marking of trees in all ways. I had no way to understand the true frustrations both of them had. It was incredibly tense. They essentially did what guys do and bumped their chests, followed by polite ignoring of each other after.

Concurrently, our youngest daughter championed the new FES. He would read to her and seemed to carry her everywhere. I can't remember if he initiated the constant piggyback rides or if she did but his ability to bond with a sweet little six-year-old was magical! At six years old, she called his parents her mum and dad too! Her logic was she was sharing her mommy and daddy, so he had to share his! His parents didn't mind a bit - I think maybe they secretly adored it! His t-shirts became her pajamas and a decade later those shirts are still in her closet. Her Norwegian mum and dad send her chocolate every year, and she's still territorial over that chocolate! A decade later and any of us could hop a flight to Norway and no questions would be asked. They would welcome us and even offer their expertise on making whipped cream! Don't laugh at the whipped cream because it is much more than buying a tub of cool whip. This was another valuable piece of information and experience I learned from hosting an FES.

Living with teenagers requires a communication level that is as different as languages. Small gaps and situations become heated when simple communication could have fixed the issue. A particular church camp comes to mind: our Fes was so angry, yet the actual issue was never discussed until it was literally time to go. He saw this group making an attempt to convert or push their religious views. This church saw a way to outreach and include the new kid - no agenda. Having a conversation about the outreach could have settled so much anger. While I won't argue religious intentions, most youth programs intentionally seek to give a safe place for teens. Their mission statement is solid, their work can and is different looking. Sometimes a youth needs a strong leader as they want a deeper connection religiously. Yet, sometimes a youth just needs a friend and those passionate to work with youth are just as happy to go skiing. Teenagers don't always see the motivation from adults the same as the adults do. I missed an opportunity to teach that boy some amazing motivational differences because I forgot to explain and communicate.

Frustrations mounted in our own home as well. It's incredibly challenging to add a teenager into your home and routine. Because I had my biological children from day one, I knew when they were hurt versus mad or simply cranky because they were hangry. I had to learn this kid's silent signals. I had to find ways to navigate his silent communication without his verbal words. I desperately needed the verbal because without it, more situations arose! My husband often goes to play poker with friends. Our FES expressed an interest in the poker game but never once said "can I go?" I also didn't directly ask if he wanted to go. Such a small communication gap created a situation of hurt. He was so very angry when he learned he was left out from going to the poker game. As the year progressed so did our communication but still there were times when basic habits had each of us frustrated, doors were slammed, and there were tears. Being kind really sucked!

In other areas communication was fluent. We shared powerful discussions, cultures were explored, engaging political conversations, economic chats, presidential debates, and lessons of prison systems. We were able to share holiday traditions and the corresponding meals like Thanksgiving Dinner. Thanksgiving is a holiday that food lovers will appreciate regardless of country. Watching never ending episodes of a 600-pound life became entertainment. We also watched a story on the largest person alive, who just happened to be found in a cave in Norway. Sweet knowledge right there, score one for America! He got his first chance to play baseball. He also got his first handful of blisters because he had not had a bat in his hand his whole life - you must toughen up that skin. He was able to drive and the reality of how easy it is for American kids to drive I learned is quite scary. Our standards here are incredibly low.

There was also the direct hit on my own stupidity. This poor soul who I was going to make all better actually came from an incredible country with rich history and a family so deep in heritage, they literally have written books about it.

The legacy he is part of is something as an American I didn't understand because I had never seen it. His love for his country at 17 was inspiring. His wisdom surpassed my own. Why did I ever think I would enrich his life? From that moment 10 minutes after we met - he was enriching mine!

Was he right in his belief that Americans are fat and lazy? Maybe, maybe not. But I was fat and lazy! I was discovering that I had filled my thoughts with fat - on how I was going to make this astute impact on his life. The reality was his life was already wonderful and he was giving me the opportunity to add to it. I had filled myself with chasing the "American dream" and forgot to stop and embrace the lessons life has. He taught me not to accept what someone hands me as proof of facts. He challenged me to learn for myself. He taught me not to sit back on what I know and to never stop discovering. He pushed me to realize it doesn't matter if the darn toothpaste lid is off - he brushed his teeth, didn't he? Within 10 minutes of meeting him he brought home how true the importance of first impressions, and how your words may affect someone. I was fat and lazy from forgetting to exercise my intelligence. Walking the treadmill everyday will help with shrinking waist inches, but to get a lazy brain going you must be willing to grow. And growth can HURT!

His dad came to visit at the end of the exchange year. Another new experience opening our home to our international families. Here's the thing about all the worries I had stressed over, they were solely in my mind! I had to let it go! Others do not care about what's under the fridge or if my laundry piles are high. They want to know me; they want to know my family! Their child just spent a year here and they are curious about us, not our ability to cook and clean. Living in an area of America where the bible belt is strong, I needed to let go of my version of Mary vs. Martha and be me. So, I was confronted with challenging myself to be less fat, less lazy, and to figure out who I am! Growth, Kind Growth, any Growth is seriously a roller coaster!

The second trip to the airport was a disaster. We had spent 10 months with this strong kid and now we just have to say goodbye. How do you truly let go of someone that you had planned to save and in return he changed your entire view on the world? You just met and must now say goodbye to his dad when you know there is so much more to discuss and learn from him?
You do it through buckets of tears, running snot, and hiccups so deep it feels your chest is crushing in. The ability to focus on what's next is almost impossible as you

literally feel a piece of your soul walk away toward his flight. I had a complete loss of emotional control and to make it worse - his dad was here to watch me break. Yep, a person I had only met a few days before got to see a truly fat and lazy American reduced into a blubbering pile of hiccups, snot, and tears! Bet he couldn't wait to get away from my kind of crazy! I completely lacked any cognitive skills that day. It was honest, but also embarrassing.

I know now that wasn't the end of our journey, it was just another lesson in growth. It takes one hell of a strong parent to let go of your own or one you consider your own. I adore every military parent, every FES parent, every parent to a traveling child, every parent strong enough to let their children fly! Our first FES, his parents knew that, I had just learned it!

Our first international son had to teach us how to be international parents - I bet he didn't read that in his pamphlet. I suppose it's appropriate that with his passion for baseball he understands the meaning of Rookie Season.

Chapter 2

Azerbaijan

2009

It only took a few days and the tears eventually dried up and when they did the desire to learn and grow more returned to me. So of course, I wanted another FES. Then my dad suddenly passed away. Our family matriarch, our go to for help, just gone in a flash. A couple of weeks later my husband's father also passed away! Just like that - no more grandpa's for my kids! In a month's time I lost my dad, my father-in-law, and had sent my international son home. It's a process to open your heart, love, and let go! As I found out, it can be a painful process at times. It's a journey to learn about someone while they learn about you (good and bad).

My dad's legacy to many is his business, but he was more than that. Yes, he taught hard! He wasn't always easy! He showed daily that to reach a goal you must be willing to take risks. I always considered myself a NON risk taker! I had started this journey of international learning - and my heart sure did take a beating that summer! Was I willing to risk another heartbreak? Was I willing to risk another loss? Did I even have any tears left? Was the overall risk worth it?

As Rookie FES returned to his home country and got re-acquainted with his life overseas, many of my own thoughts began to fall into place. I had thought letting go was forever - my only experiences with letting go were forever. I would now forever be separated from my dad. My husband and I are now truly responsible for becoming the matriarchs of our family. On the other hand, I wasn't forever separated from my FES. And I wanted to learn. I wanted to give! I wanted my next steps to be purposeful! I can't control life's storms, but I CAN adjust my sails when they come.

I did a bit of digging and found an organization that specialized with programs the US sponsored. This meant these kids received grants to come here - grants from the USA. The goal of these programs is to develop mutual understandings of each other and each other's countries. These kids didn't have the financial means to come on a typical exchange. They would be from one of the fifteen countries that formed after the fall of the Soviet Union. Their home countries are essentially even younger than the United States. The cultures of these countries intrigued me. The religious differences had my newfound love of wisdom working overdrive. The economic differences had me hooked. We had experienced a FES with a much more stable economy than ours. What would sharing our lives with a kid on the opposite side of the spectrum look like? It would require a little more training for us to be able to host a grant student. After that, the process was similar. We picked him out. He accepted. We were given the flight information and, POOF, another family member!

Did I mention he was another family member who DID NOT speak English?

You read that right!

He knew some fundamentals like how to ask for the bathroom; it was more like he knew how to do the standard "pee pee" dance and we understood the dance.

His luggage contained nowhere near what he would need for the next 10 months. He would answer every question he was asked with "Ok, ok, yes."
The exact translation for his "Ok, ok, yes" was actually "I have no clue what you're saying to me."

He would say "thank you" at odd moments, and we quickly learned the translation for "thank you" was "I don't know what to say".

He was so happy about everything, so his lack of the words was easy to downplay. While I was quickly doing an inventory of ways, I could help him master the language, our 10-year-old son was able to communicate with him just fine...we found that things like farting and burping are universal and international. We live in a small community in town, and we do have a nice yard. The FES and our 10-year-old would enjoy the sandbox, swing set, trampoline, and they would spend hours (after a driving lesson) on the golf cart. He was very hesitant about our pool because he couldn't swim. Well, it turned out he couldn't even float - putting a 17-year-old in swimmies seemed wrong but we were close!

Realizations came quickly that to meet his needs we couldn't assume he knew how to handle situations. We had to guide him with almost naive instructions. I had to continuously give myself pep talks. I would jump up and down, rotate my neck around, and say to myself "find the way!" I had to find a way to close the language gap. Finding ways to gently lead him was addicting. Once I noticed he understood something, like successfully flushing the toilet, I would quickly find a new lesson, like how we use disposable tissues! Adjusting my notions that all teenagers should know these things was challenging. American teenagers might know but he was learning culture literally from a newborn perspective and in a fun way so was I!

We went on a family road trip a few days after he arrived. The language issue lessened quickly as we learned to translate his broken English. While his first impression was discombobulating, his lasting impression would change my heart forever. Almost like the grinch, by the time this kid returned home that year, my heart grew ten times the size. My first glimpse into this sweet, kind, loving boy's heart was in the mall of America, Minnesota! There was a small child screaming for his mommy, obviously being somewhat lost. Our FES didn't even hesitate to pick the child up and hold him to his chest for comfort! He quickly found out this was a BIG MISTAKE in America! The child wasn't completely lost, and his dad went from hearing the screams of his child, to seeing a male from the middle east pick him up...we can all compartmentalize the thoughts this dad probably had. Luckily, my husband was right there and while there was some chest bumping, and security called, the situation was thankfully able to be resolved without any harm to anyone's physical bodies. However, the impact of that moment would be felt for a long time. Our FES saw a child in need, he went to aid him, he offered comfort, and was about to attempt to help the child find his parents. The father saw a terrorist, a muslim, a foreigner, and a threat! My children got to watch firsthand how one situation had two entirely different perspectives and at the core of the issue was race, religion, and culture's ugly side. As a family we were on a direct course to learn a very real part of race, things we previously thought to be just sensationalized gossip!

In my eagerness to experience the other side of the spectrum I had neglected so many possibilities. I had approached hosting a FLEX student as a bucket list and planned to check "host a FLEX student" off the list when I was done. There was no way for anyone to explain to me what I would experience with this boy because our cultures are so very different. I think any of us can assume we understand differences, but do we? I certainly didn't! That day in Minnesota was the first time I ever witnessed firsthand what hate was. I had never experienced real genuine fear like I did at that moment. I now understood an emotion many people deal with daily. I also now had a new understanding that each time I hosted a new international child my purpose couldn't be planned, but that the journey would show itself to me.

My new purpose now after this experience wasn't to rally against hate; rather, it was to embrace others' thoughts. I can't tell someone how to feel about another human based on race or culture; I can however lead by example of how easy it is to accept the unknown. I can start with the person I see in the mirror every day. We fear what we don't understand - my role could be to help others understand and, in that way, remove the fear. My "Bucket List" has a funny way of adding a couple more every time I check one off!

When tragedy strikes as humans, we have learned to view the events under a microscope. We can dissect and piece together theory or in a lot of situations piece together blame. I could easily have blamed that man in Minnesota for being racist, bigoted, or many other things. Instead, I choose to share the joy of learning something new. After a few short weeks with this boy, it was so incredibly obvious I had used much of my time dissecting life under a microscope that I was missing life at the moment. It was time to put my microscope away and use a telescope for a wider and higher view.

The challenge with viewing things with a telescope is you see bigger images. A big image does not correlate directly to big importance. However, if believing is seeing… Then buckle up because the views are going to be in technicolor!

In the year I shared with this boy I often had Batman moments. Batman moments are when the "bat signal" is calling to me. That day in Minnesota I realized a new purpose and it was like the bat signal high in the sky calling to me. The city of Gotham wasn't calling to me but the need to display and teach acceptance was. The call to teach and live a life of acceptance was now the goal. Instead of focusing on the microscopic details I chose to see a bigger issue. Details I felt needed a bigger look, a telescope look! I know it is juvenile to visualize a bat signal but over this year I had so many moments where I felt so helpless and needed that bat signal to remind me that I would make a difference. I just had to stay the course.

Early September was another painful day. I needed that signal....to remind me to think big and not get lost in details. It's not that by 2009 I had forgotten 9/11 - that day paved a new America for all of us living here - it also changed many lives around the world. As much as I want to say I felt the impact of 9/11. I did not. I watched on TV, read updates, understood new security, and my empathy was real. However, I had no actual change in my little bubble. As much as 9/11/01 shaped America: 9/11/09 had a direct applicable impact on shaping my life. My FES called from school, and I had to go get him. He was so upset, shaking, he was devastated by the things he was told at school and the things said to him. In history class they had watched a memorial on 9/11. Our FES had no knowledge, zero, none. He was so angry we would accuse "his people" of 9/11. This sweet boy had spent years dreaming of America, the free land, the opportunities here. He was so confused! That day we also learned many in our town would never accept him because his face looked similar to the photos of terrorists splashed across our screens. It's a fact we must never forget in other countries the USA wars with, they have people in their village with limited knowledge of the outside world.

35

Suppressed from the grocery store tabloids and ridiculous news feeds we see daily. At 17 years old, while studying in America, this boy learned about a war, blamed toward his faith, blamed toward his people, blamed at him. I got a crash course on hate that I didn't know existed in my small town.

I learned a new fear when adults stopped by our home and asked why we brought a terrorist to our community. Yes, community members I called friends now sat in direct opposition to my purpose. The reality is I brought this pain to this boy. I brought him here, I felt responsible for causing his pain, all our pain, and I had no idea how to fix it! I had not known people around me had such extreme opinions! The merry go round of "normal" that I was comfortable with shattered alongside my international son's heartbreak that day! How do you grow through that kind of pain delivered directly by the community you call home? You just do. Different is Different, NOT Wrong. Others who view things differently than me are as much entitled to their thoughts as I am, the goal is to accept each other not agree with each other. Learning to use telescope vision.....sucked!

In roughly six weeks instead of focusing on his culture shock and homesickness we were helping explain expressions like camel jockey and towel head. I was trying to learn on the spot how to see and explain color without judgment. I didn't and don't consider myself racist, but I learned quickly by ignoring the differences I was unintentionally encouraging separation.

Understanding concepts of white privilege, racism, bigotry, and so many other socialized words is hard. These terms are often perceived so differently pending one's own social class, color, religion, or difference. So here is my takeaway from all this: I am an American, I stand for the flag, I admire worshippers of all denominations. I believe your social emotional class is a direct reflection of your choices. I accept differences positively and reserve my right to disagree. I will keep learning and growing to be a better person and I will do so without figuratively cutting the legs off the people beside me. I do see color because those colors are beautiful, and culture filled. I will grow kindly. Accepting a socialized word isn't a liberal stance to riot and destroy! Accepting socialized words means I'm growing into a better person, and somewhere along the way my purpose and determination to accept became a passion to love better.

We calmly settled into a routine and our FES made some incredible friends. The Varsity Basketball Coach here took him on as the camera man and he held his position with pride. While the haters never left, true friendships did form, and his love was simply unavoidable. Our cultural differences were taught and learned in so many different ways. He once came home from friends so excited to tell us about this pizza he ate with round circles. Being Muslim, pork is a no-no, and obviously damage had been done. His response was "I am still alive!" So simple, so pure, and just so real! The same evening brought curiosities about the no pork rule. Many religions have something to say about pork. Researching and discovering why a rule is made helps explain some of the motivation others have. Never discredit a religious practice because you don't understand it, research it! Often the lessons of being open to researching taboo subjects leads to a clearer understanding of each other. Not judgement - understanding!

I wanted to allow this boy to express himself more, so I worked on finding ways to instigate others to speak with him. The standard question every exchange student gets is "What's your favorite thing in America"? I challenge you to answer that for yourself. Can you randomly just pick your favorite thing in an entire country? It becomes tiresome for me to hear so I can only imagine the exhaustion of a teenager. The point is we need to be smarter people who ask better questions. There are no stupid questions but there ARE questions asked out of stupidity. People different than we are, is not the issue. Our response and inability to connect with others different than us is all on us! So, for fun I began teaching all my international kids to answer that question with a more thought-provoking answer. When they are asked "What is your favorite thing in America" I tell them to respond with my name. Me, I am their favorite thing in America! That answer leads into conversations about living with host families and other relevant topics. That exchange of knowledge is extraordinary to witness. The right to exchange knowledge might be my favorite thing in living a FES life. Now, this boy took his answer to an entire new level! He wanted everyone to know how much he loved me, so much so that he often didn't even wait for others to ask, he would just say I am his favorite thing in America! Over a decade later almost every letter or message he sends starts with "How's my favorite thing in America?"

Learning to embrace his cultural differences took some re-programming for me. As a family we would get in the car, and he would attempt to sit in the front seat. No, I sit there. No, he was a man, and the man sat ahead of the woman. Constantly reminding myself he wasn't attacking me; he was acting on his "normal". I would be headed to the store, he would offer to walk me, but in front of me! Because a woman must be led in public by a man. His attempts at kindness instinctually made me want to cling to a feminist viewpoint and react. So many situations that had me micro analyzing every detail. Times when he was offering love how he knew, and I wanted to scream! Situations like when I was working with power tools, he would take them from me, and tell me it's man's work! I would be raking leaves and he would tell me to go back inside. He also learned to retreat when I would remind him, he was in America and this woman could go from zero to crazy quickly. I would lift something; he would take it from me because women are weak. Never once did he do any of these things in malice, it was just what he knew, it was/is his culture. He did these things as a kindness to show appreciation to me.

He in return learned to embrace women/girls here in America have a much more independent role. We have opinions and thoughts, and we share them. We both would get great laughs when I would tell him, "This conversation isn't going to end well for you." He didn't refuse to be open to the cultural difference, he embraced it and found that talking to females became one of his favorite things in America. This is an activity only allowed in his country if pre-approved. He would read his Koran outside to not disrespect our god, he was never asked to do this he just did. Years later he did explain better, you must be washed and clean to touch the Koran. To this day I don't think I have met another person with the heart the size of this kid. Time and time again I was reminded to put my microscope away. I found that cultural learning is about the bigger picture, not just the details. Every one of these situations brought up intelligent conversations not anger filled debates. Both sides wanted to learn about the other. Sometimes, I feel American culture has learned to circle around details, getting so dizzy we lose sight of the goal. The goal should be acceptance. Every time finger pointing blame is focused on a detail - three fingers point right back at you. The trigger finger needs to calm so the hands can help each other!

Just when I thought the hate from others was the most painful, I was wrong. This next culture lesson took me so far outside my "normal" that I struggled to make progress with acceptance.

In October, we were at a family outside reception. The kids played soccer while the adults visited inside a barn. Yes, it was a good old country style celebration! Some of our younger kids came in crying saying their sister was hurt and a few seconds later our oldest came in carrying his sister. One look and we knew, it wasn't anything a band aid was going to fix - we were headed to the emergency room as her leg wasn't straight anymore! Family members offered to take the other kids, but we couldn't find our FES. We opened the back of our vehicle and there he is, scared to the point of vomit! WTH? He refused to get out, so he rode that way to the ER, he stayed that way while we got our daughter all fixed up, he stayed that way after we got home, the next day he was STILL THERE! When we attempted to talk to him, he would scream and beg us to just send him home. He was sorry and just please send him home. It was the most bizarre reaction. We called others who had seen the incident because obviously, we were missing something. What happened at the reception? Apparently both the FES and our daughter went for the ball at the same time and when he attempted to strike the ball his aim was off, and he kicked her instead. You play hard, you get hurt hard - this happens!!! I think any soccer player knows you get kicked. We have no doubt he didn't mean to damage her leg - it was an accident! We never had considered being angry about her leg. We were concerned and we got it fixed up. Thankfully, she would live to get kicked again!

What we learned: That is not the way of his culture. A female is the property of the man. A female is soft. If you damage another man's property, he can attack, and it can be with fury. Our FES was terrified of the attack he knew was coming because he had "damaged my husband's property".

Talk about learning some culture! I do not understand the concept of property in this context. It is NOT my "normal" but I could accept that in Azerbaijan this is simply the way and I reserved my thoughts. I was clearly learning culture, one heartbreak at a time! I am so honored to have been able to learn from this young man. The risk was worth it!

Now don't misunderstand that he was some angelic presence, not everything was angelic. He was still a teenager and maybe even what we would consider immature because he truly had little world knowledge in the same content that he was unaware of 9/11. He had very simple observations that were so refreshing, but he also had the worst bathroom smells. Apparently American food tore him up. Ranch dressing was his kryptonite. And because indoor plumbing was a novelty to him, he often asked if we wanted to watch him flush. No, we, just No, we don't want to see that. One night he and our 10-year-old had engaged in a farting contest that resulted in our 10-year-old crawling out of the room waiving his white underwear in true war surrender fashion.

43

He was late for everything. His cultural habits of napping were annoying. He ate raw potatoes! He asked more questions than toddlers and sometimes I just needed a break from answering questions. I can't even count how many times I stepped on him because he would be that close, he just wanted to learn. Knowing what I know now, I want to rewind and hug him more, talk to him more, and just give him more of myself because he gave us everything he had! In the moment it seemed slightly smothering, in my reflection now it was the strongest love we had ever been given.

He lacked so much worldly wisdom and was willing to take any scrap of information you gave him. To me that makes him the best kind of human. Like many other exchange students, he of course had hoped to live in New York or Los Angeles. Big screen movies and professional sports highlight the large cities. There aren't many blockbuster movies made about small town middle America.

He also had a few celebrity idols!
Kobe Bryant was his American idol, and while his knowledge of basketball was rudimentary, his knowledge of Kobe's philanthropy and charitable accomplishments were large. So again, the FES are teaching me. I saw a Lakers Jersey. My FES saw a man, a true American legend, and

admired so many sides of this superstar! Again, I had filled my head with fat and not the important stuff! Just a musing thought in my mind, how WOULD our fantasy teams look if we formed our teams based on the character stats of people instead of their performance stats? If we spent a bit more time delving into their contributions off the clock?

While we did experience many lows emotionally through our journey with him, we also witnessed the power of acceptance. Acceptance built true friendships. Acceptance allowed us to learn how different the "breadwinner" of the family looks in other cultures. His financial situation was tight. There simply were no funds from home to be sent, or family to lean on. His dad's car had broken while he was here. No car means no work. And if the male does not work the female also loses work because the female cannot make more than the male! A man would be shamed if the woman made more money. If my husband or I lost our jobs the other would pick up the slack until we were both contributing again. Such a culture lesson!

He had to budget everything, which meant I had to budget and let me tell you I am a spoiled princess! I have never really truly had to make bottom of the barrel decisions. I have had some moments in the past where I didn't know if I was going to make rent, but I ALWAYS had family, friends, or just people to help me past whatever my dilemma was. His acceptance of dismissing things like Prom, or eating out with friends, or deodorant (yes, the struggle was real) was normal to him. He just accepted what he could do and didn't dwell on what he couldn't. No worries, we had his back...the point is it was humbling for me.

On one of his last days here, he received a grant check (which would have been nice for him to get while he still had time here to use it.) $405 was more than a lottery win to him! We went to the bank to cash it, and the teller allowed him to step behind the counter and count his own money! This is huge because he doesn't have banks like ours in his home country. She let him touch all the money and he was literally swimming in money. He still recalls that as one of his favorite memories.

When we left the bank that day he left with his cheesy smile, $405 and went to Dicks Sporting Goods where an item had been calling to him (I didn't know) that he had really wanted.   At any time while he was here, if he would have asked, I would have purchased this for him without hesitation! What was so important we had to squeeze in a quick trip before his flight ...a damn silicone $2 Kobe Bryant bracelet! That's how tight his budget and his understanding of his budget was!!!!! He never asked me for it. I would have purchased it for him! However, when the opportunity came, and he had some cash burning in his pocket he didn't hesitate. He cleared the shelf of those bracelets and bought them all. I said he understood his limits, not that he always made good choices!!!!!

My second FES taught me... "If you're ever going to find the honey, you can't be scared of the bees." Take the risk! Learning about cultures that "scare us" is essential to enlightenment. He taught me how to feel undeserved hate from others. In feeling that hate, I accepted the option not to reciprocate that same hate. I stepped out from behind my microscope and allowed myself to learn through a telescope. I chose to follow the pattern of the wise looney tunes quote: "I will kiss them and hug them and name them George."

Note: I have a niece who I am convinced has a new friend every week. I had tried for years to remember their names. My niece just has an energy for life and her acceptance of others is as natural as breathing to her. After having this FES, I gave up remembering the names of her never-ending new friends. I just call them George! Telescope learning allowed me to quit stressing over remembering details and just love the people! So, if any

George's read this book – please know you are very special, even if I can't remember your name! Should we ever meet again know, I will kiss you and hug you and probably still call you George!

He also taught me I can't help everyone, for me that was a hard blow! I know I can't literally help everyone, but shouldn't I be able to help those in my home? No, I can't. Hate is a real thing, and I can't make people not hate those I love! He helped us all grow into more compassionate people. He also taught me how NOT to make baklava! When he took his second trip to the airport, he took home Kobe bracelets for all his friends, and a piece of my heart.

Learning from a culture so vastly different yet so acutely the same... means you will have to accept and embrace Different is Different NOT Wrong. It is imperative that you learn to accept people based on their character not their culture. It does not matter what culture created the character, each of us have the equivalent to a character stat sheet and it's that data that actually matters!

Draft your fantasy team on those stats!

My favorite quote of all times, "Find out who you are and do it on purpose." - Dolly Parton

This boy was on his journey to just that - are you

Chapter 3

Germany

2009

Plot Twist

Turn of events! Thanksgiving 2009, I got a phone call to pick up a FES who has been stranded at the local airport. His host family apparently took him to the airport and put him on the next plane out. When the call came in, my husband was gone on a trip, I have 4 young children, and another FES living here at the moment. I also have no details as to what happened. Do I just go pick up this teenage stranger - knowing something bad had to have happened if he was just taken to the airport and sent on the first flight away? What situation am I potentially walking into?

After a few pages of reading this you should know - of course I go get him. It's basically empty at the airport and this boy is rather easy to spot and smell because, full disclosure here, pot stinks! I think it's a terrible smell. He has long hair, total rebel clothing, some obvious illegal habits, and eyes I simply couldn't walk away from. So yep, he's coming home with me.

Why was he sitting abandoned at an airport? A quick conversation stated ever so factual from him: He is an atheist, his Mormon host family had insisted he go to a revival with them, a few hours into revival apparently, he snapped and shared his thoughts with the congregation. Oh, to be a fly on the wall of that church! No disrespect intended to any religion - but come on - that had to have been the most awkwardly hilarious scene to witness. If you decide to host, it's important to note: These kids come on an exchange not a conversion. While encouraging FES to explore your religious practices is something I encourage, the point is for back and forth - you learn their religion consecutively as they learn yours. I am sure his previous host family had another perspective on the events that led to his quick flight. I imagine that revival was simply a breaking point for each side.

Bringing him home now means we have Christians, a Muslim, an atheist, and some not so certains all living under one roof! That same year we added some Buddhism as well but give me a minute to get there. When life gives you the opportunity to blend race, religion, culture, or any diversity don't turn down the opportunity because your proverbial table isn't big enough - build a bigger damn table!!!

I get him home and find out the next day that we are his last chance. He has had a few host families and the agency will not place him in another home. I can talk with my vacationing husband, and he agrees we will keep the new FES for a couple weeks and we will revisit the conversation of whether or not we will potentially keep him for the remainder of the year. The first week is a testament to my resolve. This new FES is a jerk! He is rude to everyone. He has no patience for the younger kids. He spends his life in front of his computer. All he ever wants to talk about is censorship, and the controls of government, and protesting both. For variety he offers to teach me how I could grow weed.

Within a week of him being here I learned more about the drug situation in my little town from him than what I had known my entire life. I now know how easy it is for anyone to get not only drugs, but chew, cigarettes, and a variety of things I am still uneducated about. I know things about this underground activity that happens around my cookie cutter life. I know what teachers, leaders, and first responders have questionable ethics and I know I will forever be grateful for such knowledge. Because......Different is Different NOT Wrong!

Reality check - if you expect that your kids and your exchange kids will never dabble, explore, or use recreational alcohol, tobacco, drugs, and casual sex - you will fail in that expectation!   Just because your small-town American church places morals and values tight as nooses on these topics does not make your viewpoint correct. It makes it different from others. We can all reserve our opinions to do what we feel is right for us, but we must not turn that right of opinion into anger against others.

He explained it best, you can never fit a round marker cap on a square marker! I don't know if he was the round or we were, but I loved him!
My husband felt the same. We agreed we would keep him for the rest of his exchange.

A new family rule went into effect almost immediately - you could believe and argue any point you wanted but your opinion had to be argued on its own merit and not by putting down others, their opinions or beliefs. Your argument must have its own merit.

The conversations with this FES were something I had never imagined. His ability to evaluate and intelligence on topics I never concerned myself with was spectacular. And man, did I disagree with every single one of them. He hated crying and thought emotion was an excuse. He had no tolerance for the juvenile parts of the younger kids. He was so intimidating in his distaste for people of position. Yet, he would turn into Ferdinand the Bull when our youngest came into the room almost as if he was curious about her innocence. He was awkward in his ability to communicate with her, but he still tried. His dry sense of humor meshed well with our oldest as well. It's important to note we picked our first international son, with hopes of matching interests. That was a failure! This kid has zero in common denominators, on paper, yet in all his differences he blended well. Don't judge a book by its cover!

How were we going to survive the remaining part of the year with a personality so full of passion? We found a balance after I smashed his computer.

Yes, I smashed his computer!

What, haven't you ever had a psycho mom moment? If not, I recommend them as they can be very therapeutic. He had used his computer and wrote a letter to my mother, and it broke the house rule of arguing your case without attacking another. If his computer was the tool to break the rule - then the computer was getting broken too. OK, OK, maybe not the best logic but it's what I went with. Shortly after "computergate" things found balance. He began walking away from a lot of arguments because he could not argue them without disrespecting something or someone else. I recommend you try to argue your points - only from positive perspectives! It's HARD!

The amount of information you can learn from each other when you have no common ground is exponential. He found some friends, and I learned more things about my town I was ignorant of. He joined a school sport and found his place.

His parents are the real deal, both are scientists, and he is an only child. His childhood was very different from small town large families. He grew up in a lab in a large city. He truly had no passion for being a FES but he had made a deal with his parents, he would survive a year to get the reward he wanted. Living with us was a means to and end for him. He had no desire to learn about us, our culture, or share himself. It is not what hosting is supposed to look like, but maybe this could be good too.

When his family came to stay it was obvious, he would refuse to label it love (because emotions are stupid in his own words) but he warmed in their presence. Similar to how he acted with our youngest. He may have often scoffed at us and refused to join conversations, but his parents knew all kinds of things about us. He had refused to participate but still listened and shared with his parents many details of his time with us.

So, did our family have any impact on him? Did his time with us add anything into his life? We will probably never know because since he left his communication has too. I haven't chatted with him in several years and that makes me sad. He's the only one of our FES with no communication to any members of our family. If by chance this book ever actually makes it into his possession, I hope he reaches out! I would love to share a warm beer with him!

His time with us taught me how easy it is to stick your head in the sand and not see what's happening right in front of you. There is no need to right every wrong in the world, but there is also no need to judge every wrong. At 15 years old this boy was more in touch with his thoughts than most adults. He was aware and paranoid of government involvement. He was passionate about the sciences of life. He found ways to let loose his inhibitions and free his thoughts. Regardless of which side of the fence you sit, he was true to himself. And, he had my computers working and running faster than they ever had! I also learned it is possible to "jailbreak" certain things in under a minute!

What I know for certain is when I see a young kid drinking, smoking, partying too much, I don't immediately think the worst anymore. I reserve my opinions in hope of connecting to that kid and possibly discovering ways to be supportive. Letting loose and having a good time is a positive thing. I would prefer the option to teach them safety and proactive steps over listing the laws they are breaking.

I do pause when I hear about a legal punishment altering the future of young adults, my heart hurts for them. As a culture we get so focused on the black and white (again the details) we forget each generation develops differently. We don't think about the effects of the punishment we hand out. In our need for control, we will ultimately have rippling effects on more than just the young person we choose to make an example of. I learned with my first exchange son; I was lazy by not teaching my children. Control isn't a lesson, it's fear.   As a culture why did we become so busy controlling that we forgot to teach? I assure you the next generations are smarter than us and our control only feeds their future power. Do we want dictators ruling us? Educating each other is where the magic happens, not controlling each other. One FES isn't going to change the laws or punishments attached, but he sure made me aware of the gray!

My third FES taught me about reaction. In the middle of many heated arguments, and there were many, he made me stop and ask myself, "What's my end game?" Do I demand dictatorship power? How will that help either of us learn? I can insert my control, but do I want to win this moment and start all over with tomorrow's argument, or do I want to win the war? I don't have to be right all the time. The statement is worth repeating I don't have to be right all the time.

Chapter 4

China

2009

Can nine people survive sharing one bathroom?   Can one home accept Muslims, atheists, Christians, and non-believers?   Can a family function peacefully when the individuals living together have opposite views on most debatable topics?

Different is Different NOT Wrong

2009 was supposed to be about welcoming our FES from Azerbaijan. Then we added the German FES. Just a few weeks after we took in our German boy, a sweet Chinese girl living in a neighboring school district was also needing a host family. This is a reality in the exchange programs. Family situations change and not all FES start and end with the same family. Not all personalities, cultures, religions, and diversities can blend! In her case, the host family had a change of jobs that required relocation and circumstances did not allow her to go with them. Her situation was in no way a reflection of her ability to adapt nor her host families. Balancing the invisible struggles of combining international elements into our normal bubbles isn't for everyone. Kind Growth takes patience and acceptance.

Obviously, I moved her in with us. These three international students from Azerbaijan, Germany, and China all ended up in our home at the same time. Acceptance wasn't going to be practiced simply in theory! Any exchange student we welcome came with some issues. Home sickness is real! Culture Shock is real! Adjustments take time! Sharing one bathroom between 9 people is a balancing act of epic proportions!

The logistics of adding another international student into our home was delicate. As with everything FES related, you just accept the challenge and figure it out. How often can you sit at your dining room table and have a meal with all your kids, and literally kids from 3 completely different backgrounds, religions, cultures, countries, heck even continents?!

And yes, it was our first international girl to live with us. I was terrified! I had been adamant that we only host boys because teenage girls have hormones, and periods, and feelings, and typically are more irrational than not. Can you imagine if my own daughters and her didn't get along? Two boys fight it out and are done. Girls are like elephants, they never forget. Ten months with girls not getting along would push the mental health limits of any house!

A little about this girl, she earned a perfect ACT score in English. She could quote on demand. Mathematical formulas and equations were child's play. She had been studying in a boarding school 13 hours a day, 11 months a year since she was five. She spoke 6 languages. Her memorization skills were entertainment to us. So why would she want to spend a year in an American High School? Academically, there was nothing we could offer her.

The education differences are vast. Not all learning comes in the form of formulas and classroom teaching. Some hands-on lessons leave the strongest memories. Creating a space for this sweet girl to express herself was remarkable to be part of. Her observance of patterns, habits, and routines of the nine people all living under one roof created lengthy conversations. She found a new voice!

We knew she would only be with us until we found another home for her, so her stay with us was brief, just 2 months in total. In that time, we taught her things like how to decorate for Christmas and spend the week together as a family. We played in the snow with no purpose other than to play. She curled her hair for the first time. She had a serious addiction to snickers in which I hope she eventually went to Snickers therapy because no human should consume that many snickers! She loved nail polish!

We learned Hello Kitty still exists and at that time was still popular. She taught me that shopping is not for the weak, that girl could seriously dent a credit card quickly! I am all about occasional retail therapy but not even I like devoting that much time to the mall!

In the short time we had her with us, we watched her study, and observed her skills. We saw her receive a perfect ACT score. We watched her win multiple full ride scholarships here in America and ultimately, she chose Boston. It's clear that the expectation China places on education from a young age is why as Americans we are nowhere near the same educational level. I can't fathom sending my kids off to boarding school and don't want to anyway but as with all the lessons FES have taught me, I think there's a meeting in the middle!

My Fourth FES taught me how I needed to take some things a lot more seriously. Today is the day to learn something new, and so is every day after today. Never stop learning.

In my observations, middle America places a lot of emphasis on skilled trades, agriculture, and common sense or life lessons. However, if this boarding school educated girl could learn to curl her hair, then we can learn a formula or two. Understanding the fundamental differences in cultures is imperative to enlightenment in all of us. Appreciating the various ways to teach and be taught makes us all better people.

Rookie FES from Norway taught my fat and lazy self how to be an international parent.

Azerbaijan FES taught me how to survive hate.

German FES taught me the value of my reactions.

Now China FES reminded me how awesome it is to teach and be taught.

All these newly acquired skills were making me a better person. Hosting an exchange student isn't something to be taken lightly. You are going to affect these kids and their families, and you will in a small way be your country's ambassador, and your life WILL be altered.   Acceptance is Kind Growth!

Chapter 5

Germany

2010

Our first adventure in exploring Germany didn't go so well. Can we ever really learn if we only try things once? I suppose that is subjective to the situation. I hiked a mountain once and crossed paths with a mama bear and her cubs. It was beautiful to see her protect them! It was horrifying to know mama thought we were the enemy. At the end of that experience, I know I don't ever need to cross a mama bear again to learn, she won! I also know my instinct is flight, not fight and the ability to hold my bladder while there is a bear snarling at me is incredibly difficult. Legit I pulled my teenage daughter in front of me for cover. I didn't need to relive that experience to learn, but this FES experience left me feeling differently, that there was more to learn.

I thought I hadn't really learned much from the first experience with our German FES culturally speaking, and I wanted to know. I have many relatives who have been stationed in Germany with tales good and bad. A few families in my community had hosted Germans. When you look at exchange profiles there are always Germans to choose from. Why do so many German kids seek exchange? The country has a few dark spots of history and like it or not we as Americans do too! Questions that intrigued me and I wanted to learn from a "millennial's" FES perspective.

2010 was the first time we hosted a FES and our oldest was the same age or slightly older. With every new international son, I think back to our "Rookie Season" and smile - he survived hell at some points! Living with us couldn't have been easy. So many rules, so much control... International parenting holds a lot of parallels to basic parenting. The first kid is always clean and shiny, with a well-balanced diet, trained to be respectful, every stop is pulled out to make the "perfect child" and then by kid four ketchup is a vegetable and they probably had a bath this week at some point. It's all good!

Having selected 2 previous students we were catching on to the fact that the data sheets collected from the respective agencies isn't always the best tool. It's a guide and it does give direction, but unsatisfied with the previous process, I decided to look at one of the questionnaires. Every agency is different, but bubble selection questionnaires do not paint a clear picture. They are generic and explain why the students we get are often very different from the brief information given. And is the USA the only country that does not use the metric system?

We wanted to attempt to get a kid with some similarities to our oldest because they would be in the same grade, and same age! Our oldest is conservative to the core. And not above using the phrase, "Well, that's just stupid." at any open opportunity. Matching that is tricky! We selected what appeared good on paper and sent in our request.

Annual background checks are done, our home inspected (we have an old farmhouse that passes inspections every year so don't ever let your home's age or style stop you from hosting if you want), now we just wait for the boy we selected to get our info. Once details are exchanged, we get to communicate with him a bit before his actual arrival and it's awesome hearing his excitement.

Picking him up from the airport it was immediately apparent we had missed one detail in his bio, he was tall, very tall! 6'5 tall! Our oldest is 6'4 so it shouldn't have seemed that much taller, but it did! We were anxious to hear him speak because we had now had two incredibly different airport pickups in terms of communication skill levels with our previous FES's. This boy fell pleasantly in the middle. It took about a day to know his happy personality did not match our oldest somber traits. A week in and I knew this kid was going to make his exchange year rewarding.

He wasn't exactly shy but certainly hesitant at first. Once he felt more comfortable you couldn't help but get cracked up by his jokes and demeanor. He had endless ways to insert humor into life. It was refreshing and light. Another family in town also had a German FES that year and we referred to them as the German Towers (both over 6'5). He seemed to make friends with him the most, which was a good and a bad thing. Good because someone knew his language and culture, bad because he didn't have to work as hard to embrace his exchange year. He found balance but this is against the rules to have two kids from the same culture in the same high school for the exact reasons I already mentioned. An oversight, I guess.

There are a lot of American flags flown around my town, around America. This was one of the first observations he made. After discussing it I learned Germans don't hang their flag, it's not exactly something they are proud of. Past wars and choices left many Germans shamed. At least that was his opinion in this case. I can never speak of entire cultures, just small parts from thoughts shared with me.

He enjoyed seeing the flags and patriotism! DO I? Do I even notice the flags flying? Have I really thought about what patriotism means? I can google it, but those words I read are very similar to when we stand for the anthem at every event or bow our heads for moments of silence. It's a programmed behavior that means what, exactly? Seems backwards, doesn't it? Here we bring these foreign kids here to teach us about their countries and he's making me learn about my own.

Everyone can level their own thoughts on patriotism. The few conversations I have had with others on this topic didn't end so well for me! Kenny Roger's song "The Gambler" comes to mind. This is a topic where I knew when to "walk away".

Regardless of where you stand on patriotism, Americans do have some dark spots in our short history. Ownership, slavery, abuse, and war are things both countries have had to overcome.   Our country did it. We righted the wrong, we regrouped, rebuilt, and made a stronger nation! That's obviously a very shortened version, but damn it! That is something to be proud of! That's the core: acceptance and perseverance will pay off. Find whatever it is that is important to you and do it. Do it well and fly your country's flag with pride! A double flagpole also flies in my yard now. My porch is decorated in red, white, and blue because regardless of whether my candidate won, or my perspective is heard, or my side even considered, I am an American. My pride is not contingent on winning a debate. America was built on people standing in protest! I believe there is a right way to protest, and a not so right way to protest. My friends aren't discarded when they no longer fit my agenda. My FES are mine forever if they will have me, even if we disagree. I may not always like America's history, but I will revisit it often with the hope of always learning from it.

We learned some not so heavy stuff too. After a nonstop week of rain, our yards were flooded, and this boy took to mud-sliding like a champion! We grabbed the sleds and tubes and made a mess out of the yard and ourselves. He might have eaten a worm but hey, its protein. It's days like that, literally filled with mud, that makes the hosting worth it. It takes time to let go of the ideology of a perfect situation and accept playing in the mud is a perfect situation.

The German American festivals we have around our hometown are not so German. We have a bakery just a short drive away that had the same name on their sign as his last name. Just a quick drive and I discovered a treasured bakery that I would never have even thought to visit if it wasn't for my FES. German was the easiest language for me to pick up, bratwurst, sauerkraut, pretzel, and wiener. Easy, I thought, I can speak German, at least when it comes to food!

He also made fun of all the drive-throughs, and he had a valid point. We spend a lot of time in our cars! Once again pointing out how lazy we have allowed ourselves to become.

Added rewards: It is so much easier to get the right apple at the apple orchard when you have tall ones along! Added Difficulties: It is so much harder to fit everyone in the car when you have tall ones! This second chance at learning about Germany was important to me. Every country has its differences and trying to compare Germans (or any 2 people from different parts of any country) is like trying to compare a New Yorker to a Cajun. It just isn't going to happen. For me I loved the differences as much as the similarities, which is why we repeated some countries. We loved learning the new and the different parts of each FES and their respective countries.

This boy was probably the easiest adjustment for our house, at this point in our FES life. He simply just blended in. He was content being part of a group and didn't need to stand out. He accepted that we share all things (even germs and the flu). He was organized with his plans and proactively asked for things so in a house of seven people he was a dream to have around! To be completely honest I like it when our FES challenges me. It doesn't matter if I get my hand held up as the victor or I am bloodied and bruised on the mat, I always learn. This kid was what I really needed that year. A calm in the storm. I had taken the risks and now he was a reward.

He had ways to just make situations enjoyable. When we brought his luggage down to prepare for his return, he had forgotten to unpack a zippered pouch when he first arrived. Out of that pouch we found over 100 condoms!!!! What exactly did he think he was going to do in America for ten months?? Regardless, with pride he said, "I will give my baby preventers to_____" (our oldest son). Seriously, how could we not laugh?

About a week after he returned home, I got a call from the local police department regarding balloons floating on the highway in front of our home. I went home to find that our youngest son had found the baby preventers and proceeded to blow most of them up and set them free out his upstairs bedroom window. As I walked along the main street with my kids and a local police officer collecting blown up condoms, I knew I would host a million times again. I also knew it would probably take months for the embarrassment of the countless calls and texts I got in regard to teaching my kids how to appropriately use condoms!

My 5th FES taught me to relax my parenting expectations. To find the fun in situations and quit trying to always learn. I know it contradicts some of the other lessons I had been learning but balance is important. I also find it ironic that my first German FES made me realize how much I dreamed of a grayer legal system and my second German taught me a gray color palette toward being a host parent.

In just a couple of years I had learned to stop demanding perfection (not that I had ever reached perfection) and choose to love all the parts of imperfect learning. I could still make divisive decisions and be rather direct in my words, but I have also learned to be ok with being wrong. It's humbling and freeing to just be able to say, "my bad" and learn and move on.

I personally found that a shift happened when I chose to ask forgiveness rather than ask permission for my FES. I accepted my FES as my responsibility, but the fear of being a rule-abiding host parent sometimes stopped me from being a good host parent. When I chose to seize moments (often without formal permission) we all were awarded more learning opportunities with our FES. The point of this shift wasn't to intentionally break a rule. Quite the opposite. The shift was to accept I was choosing to enrich their exchange with moments of embracing American family life and sometimes that meant taking a risk! To simply take a day trip the agency requires pre-planning to be done. There are request forms that need to be completed to cross state lines. For us, sometimes we just wake up and say, "Let's go here today." and that breaks an agency rule of permission. Do we miss the opportunity to adventure somewhere new because we lack the signed form or shift our thoughts and just make the decision to go without formal permission? It was those types of situations where not only did I learn forgiveness was better than permission but also more of the gray color palette I was coming to appreciate.

Note: The first contact in any issue or request with a FES is the local coordinator. I came to know mine well over the years. She would help brainstorm ideas and solutions when I was frustrated. She did our home inspections and visited the FES often while they were here. She was always rolling her eyes at some crazy thing that happened in our home.   If you consider hosting, your local coordinator is an amazing resource: USE THEM!
To my kind local coordinator, I now ask forgiveness for all the things I screwed up and intentionally forgot to ask permission for!

Example: Guns are a no for FES, they are not to have contact in any way. Guns are a hell, no! for German FES. When he inquired about how open we are in the United States with firearms I saw a teachable moment. My husband is an avid hunter, so we have many various types of guns in our home. We let him look up and down all the isles at the Bass Pro Shop and encouraged his questions and diligently tried to answer his curiosities. We even took him to target shoot. He was taught safety and care of the weapons. He had so much fun and learned some things about the differences between our countries. He also might have kept a few casings as this was a special memory he made. It was a valuable moment in his exchange as we extended a trust and an education he valued. This experience would have never been approved by the agency. We didn't even attempt to seek permission. When he was on his second trip to the airport, he might have forgotten those casings were in his carry-on backpack pocket! Apparently, security guards can be very understanding, at least from our experience they were. They must have understood the gray as well.

After we took our German boy back for that second trip to the airport, we discussed taking on another FES but ultimately decided we would not host during our own kid's senior year of High School. It was the right decision for our family to take a year off hosting.

We had time to see some of the ways we grew as a family and as individuals. I was able to observe how differently my children were being raised in comparison to just a few years earlier. How my perspective had grown and changed. I was a primate finally learning to stand on two feet and the view was incredible!

This German boy was exactly the calm I needed to really embrace what had happened to my family, what was continuing to happen within our family dynamic. He helped me realize, as a parent I needed to raise my kids not just strong enough to fly. They also needed to be confident in themselves. As always, these FES find ways to help me open my mind and see that today is so important but tomorrow's outcome balances on how we take care of today.

Chapter 6

Venezuela

2012

After a year off we jumped back into the FES world. This time in the selection process our kids were much more involved. Having the year off had made them miss it too. I made the decision to have a Spanish speaking student this time. In my mind that meant Spain. Our one son wanted a "brother." He was very specifically saying he wanted a dark-skinned brother from another mother! Now don't get your underwear in a twist, that's not a reference of racism or hate, that's an understanding of differences. Until you yourself learn to walk through life and accept life in a multicultural home, with mixed religions, races, and diversity in every conversation then you will not understand. Anyway, he wanted a brother from another mother. I was fine with adding color to our home and community, but I still wanted someone who spoke Spanish. Here's that thing again about getting lazy. Spanish to me meant Spain, I didn't even consider all the amazing countries in South America! When we close ourselves off to continuous learning, we overlook so many gorgeous things in life. I now anticipate the day I can travel anywhere South to explore.

So, my son presents me with what he feels is the perfect choice. We have a daughter in high school now and she agrees with the selection as well. In teenage girl terms her approving means, "He's Hot."

When you first select your FES, you only have small bits of information on them. After you request them, and they accept you, you get their full profile and history including full name. When we got his full profile, we all laughed. Our son had made the comment that he wanted "a brother from another mother" and it was as if this FES was simply handpicked to be our new FES, this guy had the same exact last name as us! No JOKE! The same last name!

It was time to take that trip to the airport and jump back into living the FES life!

At this point as a family, we make a game out of waiting for the kids to come through customs. As the escalator steps come down, we see legs first and try to guess if "that one" is ours." It's actually pretty easy, just look for the skinny jeans!

Here's something we learned right away; this kid was smooth! His English was accented enough to be sweet sounding. His mannerisms were very confident. He oozed politeness and he was spot on with eye contact. He also had on the tightest jeans imaginable and still walked in strut. Fashion isn't something I particularly pay attention to, I am a jeans and t-shirt kind of gal. More so, I never thought I cared, and I don't, but colored skinny jeans kind of stick out in small town living. Thankfully, fashion forward people get it and it's not an issue. Now when he walked into the local water hole where the median age is 70: he certainly turned heads! I don't think older "stuck in their way" kinda folk can decide what disturbs them more, underwear showing jeans or skinny jeans. I suppose it's a turmoil they will have to sort out on their own.

Due to scheduling conflicts and his arrival flight, we picked him up at the airport and directly went to an outdoor soccer banquet. That was a big switch from our first FES who we thought needed time to adjust. Now when we pick up our

FES, they learn really fast that we have things to do! Trust these kids to be ready, they come ready to experience America, so for pete's sake let them! Approximately 5 hours after meeting him, he was headed off with a group of kids who were also at the banquet. That's how long it took him to make friends, remember, I told you he was smooth! I knew the kids, so I was comfortable about the situation. Let me throw out a caution here that it is important to know who your FES is hanging with, especially in the beginning when you need to learn your FES and identify their silent cues.

The next day in less than 24 hours he wants to go hang out at a friend's pond. OK, maybe you stick your head in the mud and pretend "hanging at the pond" is a truism. It is of sorts but lots of other things happen at the pond! I asked our FES about alcohol; obviously legal drinking age varies from country to country and many FES have already had plenty of alcohol exposure. Of course, he positively glows with his knowledge and drink limit awareness. Our alcohol here is stronger so if you're going to drink keep in mind, less is more. Obviously, this breaks all FES policy rules. It's wrong, isn't it? However, I also know short of never allowing him to leave the house, it will happen at some point. Acceptance again is hard to truly allow to happen. I may not like all the things kids want to do and I can fight them, then they will sneak behind my back creating more issues. I can trust them to tell the truth, accept I may not always like the truth, and react with proactive goals.

 One of the hardest decisions I have ever made is the reality of practicing what I preached. How many parents have said, "call me if you're ever in trouble, no questions asked."?   How many can say they did just that with no questions asked?   The first time I picked up a child who needed a ride with no questions asked was for my own child. Not questioning was a test of will power. A few weeks later I was so glad I kept my mouth shut and lived up to my end of the bargain and asked no questions. That same child came to me on their own to discuss ways to avoid getting in that situation again!!! Talk about building communication and trust! A few more times over the years I have made the same no questions asked trip for others and my answer stays the same. I won't tattle, but I won't lie either so it's up to the individual to explain why I am dropping them off at crazy times. Explaining to a FES who barely knows me to call no questions asked is a unique predicament.

So off to the pond he goes and off I go to Walmart (c'mon, no story is complete without at least one mention of Walmart!). I am back home and putting things away within a couple hours. My youngest son comes down and says "Mom, what would you say if I told you FES was drunk?" Well, considering he only left a couple hours ago, I imagine someone must be a serious light weight. I don't say that, instead I ask him why he feels our FES is drunk? He responds, "Because he's puking everywhere!!!!" What?! Sure, enough he isn't just puking, his body is responding as he might have some alcohol poisoning. In the moment we assess the situation, do what needs done, and relax when he finally falls into a calm slumber. Now in the morning I am not so calm. I can't let this slide. If he behaves this way in the first 24 hours what the heck is the rest of the year going to look like? After he was made to clean everything, he puked on, I also made him replace the video game and shoes he damaged, and then gave two more things to do.

First, he had to call the agency and notify them of his choices. I am in no way willing to deal with criminal issues where FES are concerned. The agency puts him on probation, which means nothing more than not getting caught again. I was a little intimidated knowing any consequences were going to have to be set and enforced by me. That is another reality of FES: you get a rule bible filled with policies and rules but no real enforcement task team when violations occur. That is all fine and dandy, but if you're going to host you better have thick skin and a tough attitude because you are going to get pressed hard and often.

Second, he had to call his parents. I try to always ask myself how I would feel being the parent on the other side of those phone calls. I know we as host parents are disappointed that our FES behaved so poorly so quickly but we aren't anywhere near giving up on him or mad. Kids mess up. Character usually shines brighter after a few mud baths anyway. What did his parents say? Well, I don't know entirely because I can't make out Spanish spoken that quickly. I do know regardless of language; I KNEW he was getting a serious butt chewing and I KNEW when the bad words started flying. I think we all walked away with a solid knowledge of Spanish curse words. That's all finished and done, and I thought to myself maybe tomorrow will be a better day.

And the days just keep getting better! He was so observant of silly family habits. Things I had never thought of before, like kids poking their heads in the bathroom while I showered to tell me something they knew I wouldn't be happy about. They also knew I was in the shower so I couldn't really do anything about it until they left, and I had a few minutes to dry and dress before I went crazy on them! I often read in bed in the evenings and the kids are forever coming in to cuddle, talk, or try to make me laugh. My one son finds it hilarious to run full sprint from the hallway into my room and yell "Whale" right before he spreads wide and jumps on top of me! He apparently was Shamu in a past life. Anyway, FES caught on to this activity too and one evening they thought it would be fun to team whale! Normally this would have been a great idea for two teenagers to behave as whales. What happened instead was a full sprint run, two loud "whale" screams, an epic flattening of mom, and a loud, loud crack!

At first, we all laughed thinking for sure they just broke the bed!

Then, I rolled to survey the damaged bed and another crack, but it wasn't the bed.

A guttural scream came out of me, and I was instantly sick, the boys ran for dad and for cover. In their most adventurous whale event, they managed to jump on me just right and dislocated my hip! It was quite a scene at the doctors as I explained I was attacked by two whales! Whenever the weather changes drastically my hip will still remind me of my favorite two whales!

Learning about all that Latin culture was so much fun. Most days, this boy didn't have a care in the world. He floated from one thing to another just happy and content. Failed a test and had no worries, missed a meal and all was still good, got in a car accident and stayed cool, caught in bed with the host sister's friend and just gave that smooth smile! Yep, there it is, sex! If you can't accept that word without blushing, don't continue to read anymore.

We all know you don't mess around with your siblings' friends, as it creates lots of inter-family issues. How did our FES feel about that? The direct response was "Is there a limit to how many friends I can have sex with before any issues?" Through hosting, I have learned my FES usually tell it to me straight and painfully, as you will remember with my first FES telling me that "Americans are fat and lazy." American kids tend to search around the facts and give the answer that is truthful but not always conclusive. I had always wanted a boy FES because I didn't want girls fighting. I hadn't considered the issue of sex as my girls got older, which meant now I had girls around that were the same age as the FES! As a culture here we tend to put loads of moral pressure on sex. Teenagers quickly earn a negative reputation if they participate in any sexual activity. Parental protests are given toward condom machines in high schools. Religions even have dictates on intimacy.

Here's a culture lesson: not all cultures feel the same way! Not all people feel the same way!

Now we have a lifetime friendship damaged. A difficult discussion between families of these girls we have known for years. We also have learned some new truths. Friendships don't always look the same after FES. Families don't always look the same after FES. The goal is to allow FES to experience everything possible while in America. Parallel to that goal we had to learn to keep our family strong and communicate openly with the same honesty as FES. Our older kids were maybe a little to set to really grasp that, but the younger two jumped right on board. With that changed mindset, as parents we began to learn and accept all new realities toward our local youth. Keep in mind the boundary between parent and friend is still firmly in place but embracing an attitude of acceptance has been the hardest fought for and the most rewarding gift taught to me by a FES.

Do I particularly want to know who had sex, and where? No, I do not! However, knowledge is power, and while the details I could live without, the ability to make choices or decisions based on truths is far better than sifting through the half truths.

Do I want the responsibility of knowing alcohol will be at an underage party? Do I like my children/my FES in questionable areas? Do I understand their need for some of the dangers they naively put themselves in? No, of course I don't! I do, however, love the opportunity to teach some life lessons like never leaving drinks unattended, power in numbers, keeping locations apps open just in case, secret emergency codes, and calls with no questions asked.

My kids joke because I love too fast now. It's not that I didn't before, I just had to learn the kids/people first and I had to sift through the half truths. Now, I just jump in and love, and if relationships end, or change, I still am me. I love people where they are, not where I want them to be. If they choose to present to me someone not honest to themselves or to me, I don't judge or preach. People need to be heard. I can love you without you loving me in return.

I tend to sit on a conservative fence because that's where I am happy and content. That's fundamentally where my heart is. I can share my fence with any and all types of opinions. I shed a lot of tears when people are mean to each other simply because they disagree. My heart breaks when my own kids are mean to me because they don't agree with me.   Obviously, I don't always agree with them either, but I process, and I move on. So, I love too much, too fast, too strong! Either jump on my fence or jump off, but negativity has no place. Love me where I am or jump off. I will respect you the same!

I want to explain what I mean by the statement I made in the previous paragraph: "I will respect you the same!" With any bold statement there is room for reflection and explanation. I want you as the reader to understand what I meant by this statement. To do this I am opening a vulnerable moment, because it is in those moments that we learn.

Without sharing all the details, my family was hurt very aggressively many years ago. It was life shattering on so many levels. At the time I felt attacked by the law, the church, the community, and ultimately the person who had hatred toward me and my family. My doctor at the time was aware of the situation, and he sent me a card knowing the struggle toward healing was going to be long and hard. The card simply said, "These situations can tear a family apart, DO NOT LET THAT HAPPEN TO YOUR FAMILY!" 15 words was all it took to remind me I had power to choose my path! I chose to respect that the law enforcement team was doing their job, and I had the power to demand they help me too. The church leaders did respect my privacy and still lent out their hands in support. I had the power to reach out for it or not. The community wanted to help us. I had the power to accept it. The person who attacked us was lost in their own way and I had the Power to love them through it. Respect is a viewpoint. And a viewpoint has different sides. From my viewpoint if your intentions are positive, I can respect you the same. If your intentions are negative, then I have the power to be strong enough not to indulge you. I can love you where you are, or I can jump off. To me, "I will respect you the same" means I won't accept someone's negative progression and I respect all those around me enough not to share negativity either.

Bad things can happen to any of us at any moment. Negativity can destroy families, and as we have learned in history, it can destroy communities and cultures! My very wise doctor wrote "DO NOT LET THAT HAPPEN TO YOUR FAMILY." I can respect you by sharing positivity. And, I have the power to respect you enough to jump off your prospective fence if your direction is negative.

A FES life has truly taught me it really doesn't matter what I think, what matters is how I treat people. I get so very very tired of complainers, complaints, and finger pointing blaming.   I just care that you're a decent human and everything else will work itself out. I am always a decision away from changing my life and the lives of others.   I choose to give in any way I can, even if others say I love too fast. Venezuela FES helped me see that by reacting quickly I often made large mistakes. When I adapted some of his laid-back swagger, I was able to look at situations rationally vs emotionally and respond to them instead of reacting.   Considering another's emotional well-being before sharing my version of a soul purging truth takes practice and patience but everyone is worth that from me. I am worth that from me!!

This particular FES, our 6th one, was now ready to take that trip back to the airport. He had a year of friendships, adventures, love, and crazy. He was youthful through and through. He didn't apply much pressure on himself. He was fun! He taught us the art of making arepas and canned meat. He called his sister a "rent" because she cost too much, like paying rent. He had smiles and positive words for everyone he met. I wanted him to speak Spanish. Our son wanted a brother from another mother.

We got a friend for life!

We also had an airport full of tears. I had fought hard since Rookie FES not to cry at the airport. I should have known my smooth talking, sweet-worded Venezuelan was up to something weeks before. He had paid particular attention to my charm bracelets. I shared the story of them often. Well, he was literally in the metal detector at the airport when he beeped. That beep set him running literally! He left his items on the conveyor belt, rushed past security, literally jumped over four sets of ropes, ran right up to me, and while full of tears he wrapped his arms around me. He is simply crying in my arms, and yep, that means I am crying too. So is the family and so are the security guards watching this spectacle. A few strangers have stopped to watch this black teenager cry in his white mama's arms. It's one of those moments you know has a huge impact on your future but you're not sure what that impact is. He eventually collects himself, and hands me a Venezuela charm for my bracelet. Then flashes me that signature smile and says, "Don't forget me, mama", and then he is off again, jumping the security lines to get back in place and retrieve his items.

He taught me that it's time we put more value on love and friendship. Not every relationship or situation has to be "heavy" to be good. Enjoy people right where they are!

A year later he returned to visit. He simply wanted to be back home in America for a few weeks. He also shared so much more about his home country. Like most kids he wasn't aware of many things going on around him in his government local and nationally. He wasn't aware of the pending poverty in places and living conditions of many. After being separated for a year, he was shocked by how much he saw when he returned to his natural country. This new information weighed very heavily on his heart, and he had mountains to share and unload on me. We literally sat around our fire an entire night, and we watched the sun come up together. The way his heart reached out to me was the reason why I host!

There are no words to describe what it feels like to be needed in such a powerful way, to have an 18-year-old who wants advice and direction from you. As a mother I have noticed my own kids start to pull away by that age. Ready for an independence they aren't aware of yet. This young man wanted my knowledge. He wanted my direction. I do not feel equipped now, nor did I then, to offer that knowledge. He sat and listed event after event of his year with us. Starting with that early drunken stupor. He cataloged events in a chronological order, and he told me the lessons he learned from me. I mean WHAT!!! He listed things like integrity, self-worth, responsibility, empathy, and trust! He felt I taught him those things. Now, I don't feel I taught him those things, but maybe I reinforced them. International child, biological child, friend's child, or a stranger, I believe this FES experience should be a motivation for all of us to leave that kind of legacy to the next generation. Have the confidence to be you and love well, and the legacy will follow!

I want to leave a legacy. Heck, that's why I started this book. This FES took time to say to me directly that I had left a legacy. The knowledge that I helped him; I can't explain the feeling with that. I can tell you this: if someone marks your heart TELL THEM! Don't let moments pass without sharing with each other the value they have in your life. Like my doctor, be bold enough to send a card - it may change someone's life!   Bad things are going to happen, and you have the power to heal yourself and others.   Get mad if you must.   Be sad!   Then exercise your power to make a difference in your life and in the lives of those around you!

I love music and I have a song that I pull out every time I am feeling less than. Nicole Norseman's *I Wanna Leave a Legacy* is that song, and this boy made me feel this way! It doesn't get much more powerful than that. I truly hope he knows just how much I loved him.

It's also why we should never fundamentally try to change anyone. Wear your skinny jeans in the country! Love who you want to love. Democrats can love republicans. Conservatives can love liberals. Black can love white. Rednecks can love princesses. Christians can love Muslims! Love can win! We will each grow in our own time. We can share a level of respect with those in opposition of our beliefs!

Different is Different, NOT Wrong!

He never really stayed in his home country after that summer he returned to visit. He studied at a university abroad. Of course, he went home for visits. His parents split their time between a couple countries. Due to additional turmoil in his country at one point it just wasn't safe to return. He never let my birthday pass with our acknowledgement. He always had random questions. He was a free spirit yet so grounded in life, in love. He was probably full of shit most of the time, but I loved hearing his voice when he would call. I always looked forward to his crazy stories and tattoos. He was an extraordinary example of living life to the fullest. I imagine anyone who ever met him found a reason to smile!

In the fall of 2019, we lost this young man. He passed away alone in his apartment. A harsh reality of life is death. He wasn't our child by birth, but he was our child by love. Treasure the moments you have with each new person in your life. Accept them where they are. Allow yourself to leave a legacy!

Chapter 7

Norway

2013

There was never a doubt I wanted as much exposure to
Norway as possible! Rookie FES was a game changer -
pun intended! In 2012 our entire family traveled to Norway
to visit Rookie FES and his family. Ice cream and cakes
were everywhere! Not only did his immediate family
welcome us, additionally family friends allowed us to use
their home while we stayed. YES, complete strangers
allowed us to live in their home for weeks, no contract, no
security deposit. We walked behind waterfalls, saw snow
in July, stood on the Fjords, caught fish off rocks in the sea,
made aquariums, drank to-go coffee with no lid, stood on a

cliff, sailed on a crab boat, caught crab, and found a new passion for art. We watched tourists come and go, admired the open fish markets, trolleyed to the top of Mt Floyen, and bought ridiculous Norwegian souvenirs because we all wanted the memories to last.

While in Norway, we were amazed at how quickly locals caught our American accent and descended on us with decorated questions about America. It was a game of "poke" at Americans for information as they were curious about our culture, government, and us personally. The news really doesn't give all of us around the world great presentations of our true selves. We got a real-life taste of how our FES feel here when we blast them with absurd questions.

Moments that instantly showed me I had made progress growing yet had a long way to go. While standing on the edge of a cliff with my husband watching a race in the water, I was cautious about where exactly to stand.
I asked my husband, "Do you think we can go all the way to the edge?"
A native smiled and said, "you can go as far as you want, just maybe don't fall off."
At that moment, I had a flashback to my Rooke FES saying "want honesty?"

We chatted with this man a bit and learned his son was also in the race. He apologized if he came off rude, followed up with, "sometimes we get so busy following guidelines set by others that we forget to use our own intelligence."

A polite smack in the face for sure! In all seriousness we have completely allowed ourselves to have a herd mentality. We wait in lines at theaters, amusement parks, toll booths. We walk around caution tape and no trespassing signs. At sporting events and concerts the traffic flows and we follow. The road less traveled is almost a myth. Here I stood on this cliff, majestic scenery everywhere and I for real wasn't sure how far I could go because I had no boundary, no caution tape, and no one telling me my limits! It was a sad reality, I mean - I know - not to go so far as to fall off the side of the cliff, but I was still waiting for someone to set my limit for me. When did I forget to use common sense? Why do I allow others to set my limits? I am not talking about vigilante justice, or rebellions, but just basic decision making, limit evaluations, and self-control!

Another Fantastic Example: Every coffee shop coffee I have ever purchased came in a disposable cup with a lid that says caution contents are hot. Those who know me well know I go to A LOT of coffee shops! I leave with my java and throw the disposable cup away when finished. In Norway, when I got a coffee to go, they served it in a ceramic cup with NO lid! I looked at the cup for the words "caution contents are hot" and they just weren't there. I followed the lead of the family, guiding us, leaving the shop and continuing our walk, with no lid, no temperature warning, and realized I could do this! I could walk without a lid telling me the contents in my cup are hot! Then, they tell me, we will return the cups later! Yep, you heard me, return the cups and here's the shocker: PEOPLE DO return the cups! Containers are placed outside business doors for returns after business close. Mind blown! It's not that I was incapable of drinking and returning this reusable cup - it was the reality that I had never even considered it. Again, just accepting the status quo and not using my own common sense.

Another few more examples won't hurt! It was raining one day while we were out, and the family we were with walked right into a hotel and asked to borrow some umbrellas. We weren't staying at this hotel, yet she walked out with umbrellas for us to use and return when finished. No $ exchanged hands and when finished we returned them! Parks had heaters for you to turn on and use, blankets draped over benches, and games on pavilion paths. All these items were there for you to use and then return as you found them. All these things would be stolen and pawned within 10 minutes where I live and less than that in the big cities. They practiced self-control without a sign or lid to tell them to! I want to live like that.

We have so many clean, new, powerful things and places here in the United States. Take pride in going to your local zoo, marvel at the top of some of the world's biggest roller coasters, and embrace what Thanksgiving means. Appreciate the mountains and the large open plains equally. Respect your leaders, vote differently next time if you don't like who is in office, but while they are in office give them the respect they earned, exercise your freedoms! Respect others have the same freedoms. Allow yourself to love your country.

Getting to view another country through an actual family living there was an education I will always be grateful for. No tourist stuff (ok maybe a little), but experiencing actual homes, routines, and real people. I also got to dip my feet in the other side of the Atlantic!

When I got a chance at another Norwegian FES I didn't even read his profile, I wanted him!

Of course, I had built this country up so much I wasn't leaving much room short of perfection.   He got off the plane, spoke decent English which is always a huge relief. Remember just because their profiles say ** years of English, it doesn't mean they will actually speak it well.

He shared a room with our middle son. Another decision you will need to make as a family is whether to allow them their own room, or to share a room. I prefer them sharing, because they will have a lot of moments where they try to hide. Having a roommate makes them suck it up, process what they are feeling, deal with it, and move on. I am not negating culture shock or homesickness, they both can be debilitating to a teen, I am just speaking from my experiences.

FES quickly made friends with the same group of boys our Venezuelan Fes hung out with.   If I didn't love this group before I did now. Acceptance - this group of boys welcomed another one of our FES into their group. Friendships are important for a FES to develop while here, your Fes will always remember their host families, but adding friendships strengthens the entire exchange. If they make powerful connections to kids their own age, that's where the magic happens. Allowing youth to connect internationally opens our future in exponential ways. You can't force it, it's organic, and it's accepting! Many of these boys from this group eventually graduated high school and honored our country, and honored us, by enlisting in various branches of the military. I have no idea if exposure to FES encouraged those choices, and it doesn't matter. I am honored to have known them and for a short while and enjoy their kind hearts. I still see a few of them from time to time and adore the men they have become! Thank you to every military hero! To this group of young men here in my community that embraced the FES life you are my heroes, both for your military bravery and your exceptional souls!

While every FES comes from various financial backgrounds, it's not our business to know and you're encouraged not to have anything to do with their finances except to help them budget if required. We are a solid middle class, both parents work, we get mud on our clothes kind of people. I count it homemade if I opened the package at home, and the men folk have no problem shooting snot rockets in the winter. There are so many things that can create struggles between a FES and their host family. Money should not be one of those causes but it can happen.

This particular Fes had an endless supply of money. He had a package delivered which I opened. I learned quick in

FES life that packages are not always what they seem. Example: Pringles cans hold 7 cans of chewing tobacco. School books can hold a small liquor bottle if you cut the inner pages out. Teenagers are crafty; don't underestimate them. This package he received was large, but light. Our FES had been complaining about how cold it was in NOVEMBER! The irony of a boy from a Nordic climate being cold here. The package contained a winter coat. An $800 winter coat! I have never spent $800 on a coat. After it arrived, he didn't even like the coat, so he never wore it!

He really had no restraints on his spending, and this created another new issue. How do you justify one kid purchasing $800 jackets when the others living in the house can't? It is easier to bond if everyone in the home has the same standard. He was not about to limit his spending, so I had to choose if I was going to allow it to create a negative lesson or a positive one. It is possible to learn acceptance when things aren't in your control. So much can change in your life if you replace resentment with gratitude.

He went out to eat 5-7 times a week. He wasn't a fan of our food (our house food: not American Food) so if he wasn't eating out, he would walk to the store and purchase whatever processed, sugar filled, plastic wrapped item suited his fancy. Faced again with the same argument of how is that fair? FES eats pop tarts and Mt Dew for dinner while the rest get chicken and broccoli. Sure, we could have drawn a line in the sand, but the knowledge of knowing we alone would be responsible for the execution of any discipline is enough to give us pause and ask, "What is our end game?" We get these kids for 10 months! It's not our job to raise them. It's our job to share, teach, love, and direct them. We share what we can, we teach what we know, we love them where they are not where we want them to be, and we do our best to direct them, but we don't force them to do anything (safety issues notwithstanding). Due to his diet his acne was out of control, and I know his parents had concerns but with unlimited cash flow he had access to whatever he wanted.

Academically he had no hardships. Most FES get better English grades than our American kids. Math is often not challenging because formulas and equations are memorized at very young ages. Most FES speak more than 2 languages, while American kids unless exposed by family have limited knowledge of outside cultures. We recommend kids take US History. My FES have been very disappointed in the content because they already knew what was studied. Physical education is an easy class for

FES to be interactive and learn more about local teen behavior.   He was a very easy to get along with kid.

He played soccer in the fall, then wasn't particularly interested in sports after that. Which was ok because he had made many friends and he still went and supported his host siblings in their events.

In the Spring his family came to visit. His dad communicated well as did his sister. His younger brother was a fiery thing. They treated us to dinner at FES's favorite place, Buffalo Wild Wings! Sports bars were certainly this FES's favorite. They were also beyond excited for no line outside of Abercrombie and Fitch. His family stayed at a hotel about an hour away so the disconnect was difficult to form relationships around. I am so glad I got to meet them; I just wish I could have got to know them more. A few months later, his aunt and Grandma came for his graduation. They sat through an incredibly HOT outside graduation! His aunt had been a FES herself many years ago and hearing her perspectives gave me hope. Hope that even though every situation with FES was far from perfect, not all storms leave destruction, some storms leave beauty.

Gathering things to say about this particular FES is difficult. He was very spoiled and self-centered. He didn't pay a lot of attention to any of us. I never felt he didn't like me or us, he was just lost in his own circle. Both of my Norwegian boys have now been standoffish but where Rookie was curious, current FES was complacent. This isn't a stat sheet comparing boys, just a reminder teenagers are teenagers no matter where in the world they come from. I don't know why I ever thought two boys from one country would be similar. After all, even the kids I raised in the same house are all different.

When the time came to take FES to the airport, I was indifferent. I was glad to have met him and learned some about him, but I really didn't feel the year changed either of us. We said the obligatory "see you soon" and left the airport. I spent some time pondering where I went wrong? He's a great kid, he made amazing friends, why didn't we connect? Should I have fought harder to limit the spending?

I cleaned out the FES room as soon as I got home. I went from indifferent to flat out pissed. I was no longer pondering my missteps- I was now counting my stair steps after multiple trips full of bags and then construction repair garbage!!!!

All those trips to the store totaled up to quite a pile under his bed, in the closet, and stuffed in drawers:

54 folded up empty pop boxes = 648 pops

12 pop tart packages = 96

32 empty chew cans

2 full chew cans

A handful of monsters, little Debbie boxes, pringles, candy wrappers, and misc. other snacks

He was only here for approx. 300 DAYS!!!!

But that's not the worst of it: all down the wall beside his bed were stains. He literally sat in bed at night and spit down the side of the wall, ruining the wall section, the carpet, and the mattress! Holding back the vomit wasn't an option! That's not even all, I said full disclosure, right? Among the piles of garbage were piles of tissues and one already used personal satisfaction device! That's right, ladies and gentlemen, he left his dirty friend behind for me to dispose of!

I wanted to be mad at him. I was mad- and then - I couldn't be. In discovering his left behind treasures our family bonded over the cleanup and remodel of that bedroom. He was a kid, with unlimited cash flow, parents' oceans away, and an American host family who refused to entertain the entitlement attitude so he sought his fun with what money could buy.

A month later he messaged apologizing for being such a jerk!

He acknowledged that he had behaved selfishly toward our family, the community, and the experience. A year later, another message, a similar more evolved explanation of his year here.

Seven years later, he reached out wanting to help and be supportive in a very intense period not just in our nation but his as well. He wanted to thank us! He wanted to visit! He is a man now. The best kind of man. I know now, we mattered to him then and still do today. He wasn't really ready as a teenager to listen, but he heard and as a man he had his own growth. If I had held on to the resentment, I would have lost the ability to be grateful for knowing how mature he became.

Lucky 7! What did I learn from him? If you're going to see the rainbow, you're going to have to stand in the storm. Storms can leave destruction, but sometimes you're lucky enough to see the beauty it left behind as well.

Thank You Lucky seven!

When you reach that breaking point, when life is not fair, when you are disgusted past your wildest imagination. Just breathe. Focus on your end game. Believe in that legacy you have been trying to leave. Then go stand in the storm and find the rainbow.

Fes #7 taught me to chase the storms!

I think it's important to note at this point that when a particular story I write points out some real-life challenges, it's not negativity coming from me, it's the lessons of my journey! Yes, it's my perspective of the events of the exchange year and certainly there is another side. I would not trade a single experience with any of these kids. The way I learned to accept the lessons and make myself grow is an unreturnable treasure. Choosing to embrace growth has had its painful moments, both for me and for my FES.

Chapter 8

Germany

2015

In 2015, we had another senior! With so many incredible moments and important future decisions we do not have FES during our kid's senior year. Our senior daughter is pretty set, she has made her decision for college, her grades are fantastic, she overall is ready to take the next step. The fall term (2014) is full of all the highlights every student deserves. Then, shortly after the new year we are asked to consider taking on a FES for 30 days. There are programs that allow students to come stay with an

American host family for 30 days to see if doing an exchange for an entire year is something they would want to do.   Our daughter was excited about it and agreed she was set for the "next steps" so having a FES here for a month wouldn't hinder her process.

We welcomed our "sample FES" in the spring! We expected little more than potentially meeting a new friend because truly how deep can a relationship form in 30 days? We think he was a FES anyway, because he sure looked a lot like Niall Horan from One Direction.   Seriously, he was approached a couple different times in stores and random places for his autograph!!!

On top of everything this boy taught me, I also learned about a band I didn't know existed prior to meeting this young man.

And how to quickly get in the car and leave a public place. I am not entirely sure why people would think the famous Niall would shop in Joann fabrics, maybe it was his hair flip!

Fame and paparazzi aside, this young man was an open book. He preferred a vegetarian diet and family dinners. He was born in Russia but due to poor air quality and failing health at not even two years old, his family packed up and headed to Germany in hopes of keeping their young son alive. Grip onto how that would be for a moment: You have a baby which should be a joyous time and then he is so ill, unable to breathe, and you know from professionals and research this baby will only thrive if he is removed from his current environment. You make the decision, put the wheels into motion, and leave your home country. You leave your language, your heritage, your family, your LIFE for him!

This wasn't the same as an exchange year, this would be forever. I never did meet his mother, but THAT is what motherly love and sacrifice look like!

Many countries are similar to the United States in various levels of diversity. Much like the United States, not always are the differences equally blended. Make no mistake, if you live in America, you should speak English. If you live in America you should stand for the national anthem, respect the flag, admire lady liberty, and you better grill out every Memorial Day, 4th of July, and Labor Day! Thanksgiving should be EXACTLY that, a time to be thankful for all things encompassed by the red, white, and blue! Experiencing diversity will make you more considerate of the needs and perspectives of others.

While all nuances of diversity, race, religion, and culture should be accepted and embraced, that does not hold any country accountable for exceptions. If you leave one country for another you make that new culture yours, you do not ask that new culture to make exceptions for you. I tell every FES without exception that they will stand for the anthem. I do not ask them to sing it, or memorize it, or practice it. I expect them to do exactly what they came here to do: embrace American culture.   If a team stands, you stand! If a team prays, you close your eyes and sing kum ba yah in your head for all I care, but you participate in the action that means so much to many! No exceptions - just acceptance. Accepting that there is a place for every culture, diversity, religion, wealth, and intelligence is at points suffocating. Your opinion is one of many, valued for sure, critical to you, important to many, but not always what is best for all. Be part of the solution, not part of the problem.

Why are we so quick to accept those we closely interact with and ignore those who don't impact our daily lives? As spouses we understand that we may not always be able to win every argument, so we compromise quickly. As friends we understand "bad days "as we all have unique differences, so we excuse a nasty word or missed acknowledgement. As parents, we learn quickly every meal doesn't include liked vegetables, yet we diligently work to find positive ways to encourage future vegetable tastings.

So why do we continue to fight on topics of no win? Abortion, gun control, climate, democratic/republican? We make ourselves and our country look like idiots every time we can't do a basic thing like accept each other. These topics are important and situations dire. There is no argument that will settle any of these heated topics for everyone. When compromises are made where will you be? To quote Thumper's mom," If you ain't got nothing nice to say don't say anything at all!" If you're honest with yourself, can you accept the compromised agreements in a positive progressive way?

This mom delivered a baby in Russia, lived in very uncertain conditions, the health of her baby was in danger, then she ultimately traveled countries away from home to keep her child alive and safe. She found an area in Germany well populated with Russians there for similar reasons. She soon had a network of Russian friends inside German boundaries. She learned the German language, and this boy grew up speaking German. She accepted her choice to move to Germany, she didn't ask the country to make an exception for her. She followed the immigrant requirements and respected Germany as it was now her home too. This boy is still very aware of his Russian heritage and legacy. He listed German as his native language and could also speak several other languages including Russian. She accepted the compromise she decided on and ventured forward without negative recourse. I am certain she had plenty of things to worry over, but she fought the good fight and made sure her family basked in the positive. She is an ambassador for immigration. Sometimes I feel terms like immigration, alien, illegal, or visa are simply interchangeable when they are all very different.

Albert Einstein knew the secret to diversity living/learning. He states in a famous quote of his, "I never teach my pupils. I only attempt to provide the conditions in which they can learn."
I talked earlier about how my children will say I "mind fuck" them. I don't think I do. I am simply doing my best to place them in conditions in which they could learn.

When we attempt to blend and mix cultures neither side of the fence is ever going to truly understand the other, but we can provide conditions where we both can learn.
This mom created a new life. She provided the conditions for herself and her family to learn something new. Years later this boy wanted to check out America and she encouraged his passion to learn about other countries. She knew from experience the benefits of learning new

cultures! As a parent, a leader, she made the sacrifice needed, and miraculously didn't come out bitter or jaded. She accepted her new home, embraced its culture, maintained her legacy, and created conditions for her family to learn positively.

Why the hell can't we do that?

We have 50 gloriously diverse states. Yet we put more energy into competitive college border battles than acceptance. We have a surplus of propaganda supporting causes important to us but not so much to others. If we spent even a fraction of our presidential slander money on positive support, can you imagine?

In 30 days, a Russian born German boy and his mom made me feel so ashamed. While I had already begun the process of acceptance and pride in patriotism, I hadn't placed sacrifice in the same dialogue.

117

If you don't like your situation, change it.

If it's unsafe where you live, move.

If you are intimidated, be strong.

If you are feeling bullied, find confidence.

You have the power to change your life. Accept that and don't ask someone else to carry your burden. Every school across the nation will probably want my silence on this next statement: I truly feel bullying is one of the worst words we ever added into our school's curriculum. We made it acceptable to be a victim. We made it empowering to blame others for our hurt. Mental health is critical, but the pendulum can't sway just one way. We must prioritize the power within ourselves, not only the hurtful outside forces. Forms of perceived bullying will always be there in every stage of life. We can't give control of our happiness to outside forces. Mental strength and toughness play a huge role in mental health. Teach that! Teach personal accountability, perception, confidence, and strength. That lesson takes the power away from any bully!

"Find out who you are and do it on purpose." - Dolly Parton

Remember the household rule my first German taught us: "You can argue any point however you want but you must argue it on its own merit and not by putting something or someone else down!"

I already crossed the boundary in this chapter by getting preachy so a little more won't hurt.
We live in America, we are free to vote on topics, people, laws, and so much more. If you don't know how to find your own power, start with your birth given power and right to vote! You didn't have to migrate here, it's your birth privilege. Show up and be heard in a positive way. Your voting side won't always win but you will have made the choice to be heard.

I titled this book Kind/Growth and I meant it. 30 days was all it took for this young man to impact me so greatly. Every time I open my heart to a new experience I learn. I might have learned as much from My 8th FES in 30 days then I learned from others in a full exchange year. Shame was a new emotion for me, and I didn't like it much.

Acceptance is so incredibly difficult, and now I learned forgiveness to myself is painful too!   Sacrifice is vital to growth and growth sucks! The journey of being kind for 30 days seems so easy. And it was, but boy did the growth part hurt. It shames me to admit I have never sacrificed for anyone the magnitude this mom did! She sacrificed and then led with grace. I hold this One Direction look-alike boy as a challenge to myself to hold myself accountable, and to raise my kids aware of our responsibility to accept the sacrifices others make.

I learned not to overlook the sacrifice someone is making because it doesn't benefit me. I accept that their cause is just as vital as mine. My journey is so important, but I must travel my journey without lashing out at others. We are all in the same river, just in different boats!

For whatever reason when I think about this mom I think about a story from my teenage years. Another walk into my past that again was a lifetime lesson. I promised full disclosure and how can I really acknowledge my growth or share it if I don't take a few walks into the past? This is a story of triumph because once again a brief moment changed my direction!

I was barely fifteen years old, drowning in tears, all alone watching the water ripple at the local reservoir. Earlier that day my secret had gotten out. The secret I was petrified of. I was pregnant. 15 and pregnant! It had only taken a few hours from my initial admission for the news to reach many directions and I was devastated. What was I going to do?

I had hidden it for six months!!! My future seemed to have changed simply by the acknowledgement from others. When I was hiding the pregnancy, I suppose I could pretend it wasn't really happening. I was scared because this pregnancy had just become real. I was officially "that girl" and adding to the negative statistics of teenage choices. All I could envision was dropping out of high school and calling Jerry Springer to be the next tabloid talk show guest!

What does a fifteen-year-old kid know about becoming a mom? I sat for hours crying, thinking, and not coming up with any real direction or plan.

Then, a much older man sat down beside me. I didn't know him. He just sat there and offered me a reusable hankie, the kind only a grandpa carried, it even had the cute cross stitching! He told me I didn't need to talk to him, he just didn't like seeing me seem so alone. How did he know how alone I really felt at that moment? Then he told me something powerful: "You can't control life's storms, but you can always adjust your sails." That's what I have been doing ever since. That baby boy was a beautiful 10-pound 6-ounce, red faced, fat little sumu looking miracle. That baby boy and I had a lot of growing up and adjusting our sails together. I graduated high school and never did call Jerry.   He is now a teacher affecting the lives of so many young children.

A FES life gave me an opportunity to continue adjusting my sails. This Russian /German mom did too!

Years later, I read that quote spoken to me from the man that day at the reservoir. I learned that Dolly Parton said that! She also said my favorite quote mentioned throughout this book, "Find out who you are and do it on Purpose." Coincidence, or a perfectly timed opportunity? This man changed a part of my life that day. I don't know who he is so I can never have that chat with him. But I want him to know, I heard him, and I have been adjusting my sails since.

Sometimes, I wonder what that man would say to me now.

My 8th FES taught me the value my journey could have. I must make the hard choices and hold myself accountable to the effects of those choices. He left me feelings of shame, knowing that through my own personal sacrifices I could do better. His family showed me how powerful it is to make my decisions for myself and accept all repercussions. No one has the power to make me feel less than unless I give them that power.

I have never met a bully big enough to knock me down! You can be strong in your own self and make a way that you too will never meet a bully with any power over you! Sometimes situations suck! Sometimes people suck! Do you let the storm take you out? Or do you adjust your sails?

Chapter 9

Republic of

Georgia

2015

After that emotional 30 day beat down, I was ready to dive in again. I adored my first FLEX son (students from the countries that formed after the fall of the Soviet Union) and I emotionally needed to give and be given that kind of simple love again. My first FLEX FES sucked so much joy out of every part of life. I was very wrong when I put that expectation on a new FES.

I feel hosting gave me the unique perspectives to appreciate so many new different ideologies and logistics to life. It did not however prepare me for a kid to not like me! We had hosted a kid before who didn't like anyone, so it was easy to be in a flock of unwanteds, but to be singled out was a new twist.

Blending culture and family must be an exercise in willingness to find equalities. Some people are born to embrace and adore cultural differences, others are curious and respectful of cultures but have no desire to compromise. And yet others, no matter how much effort is applied, fail to find common denominators. All variances of culture awareness are understandable. Within the exchange programs however only open acceptance can be tolerated. My experience with this boy fell into the latter, with no compromise and we spent the entire exchange without a common ground.

It begins as always by making that first airport trip again. We only have 2 teenagers living at home now, so the craziness is less. We know from his profile a few things but nothing too deep. He has a love and passion for martial arts, which will be an issue as in our area we don't have a lot to offer in that art, but we will discover what we can for him. At first sight his smile is bright, and he genuinely seems pleased to be here. He is very engaged talking to my husband and son but not so communicative with the females. I always love noticing who a new FES seeks for comfort. Watching for those silent communication skills each of us have, and I learned after Rookie FES, I must search diligently for! It was easy to see his comfort around my husband. I would have to wait to find my place in this new FES's experience, and I didn't have long to wait.

The discomfort started immediately! Our first meal together set the scene for the next ten months. He wanted meat, meat, and more meat, and we simply don't eat like that. Of course, meat is served at most meals but not all. Depending on the schedule, popcorn from a concession stand might be dinner! He quickly taught us about a cultural feast called supra. A "Supra" is a type of feast that culturally sounds amazing. The influences of flavors from Greece and the Mediterranean and add in a hint of Turkey and Persia and no doubt the supra is an experience I would love. Now, he didn't expect a supra at every meal, but he wasn't impressed with my offerings either. He was direct to point out he needed more protein, and I should have more meal options available to him.

The inadequacies I felt were deep, I wanted to make him comfortable here, but I was failing to meet his expectations.

The disappointment he felt stemmed from his expectations of how a mom should be. He expected me to treat him like the women in his family treated him. As the only son he was loved and cherished. He explained it as pride for the women of the family to care for the males. I saw my role as a mother very differently. I expected him to embrace the American way or my American way. I felt he was here to experience an exchange, to learn and observe a culturally different way. Sadly, we would both lose. The battle lines were clear from day one.

He did great with school. He quickly made some friends and joined the football team. With his love of martial arts, he was naturally a fighter and had to be reminded a few times that even in a sport as physical as football there are rules and guidelines for contact. In the winter he wrestled and again that natural fighter in him had to be reined in for wrestling. He did make a connection with someone in the martial arts world and was able to enjoy a few classes and events in the martial arts. He was rather focused and often could be found in the yard doing various workouts. For movie junkies it was reminiscent of Roadhouse when Patrick Swayze would exercise in the yard. He could spend hours just in various poses and stretches. He was very disciplined in his workouts.

The most wonderful thing about accepting culture is acknowledging the positives and negatives in your own culture. Often the pressures are so powerful to make others understand one another. We want our point of view heard! We forget, we do not always need to understand each other. We need to accept each other. I myself was raised by a very dominantly sexist father and a homemaker of a mother. Some might say she was subservient to him. And what is wrong with that, absolutely nothing. It worked for them! My childhood was filled with lessons and comforts many never get! I don't care who wears the proverbial pants in the family as long as the pants get worn.

Now, I am way too outspoken and often too demanding to handle anything less than a partnership. My husband has to put me in check often. I don't like when he's correct and I would rather chew on crud than admit defeat in any argument. We both work so all house chores, schedules, and activities fall on to each of us. We must communicate, or chaos descends. There is nothing wrong with equal partners. There is also nothing wrong when one or the other partner is the visual leader. We again are all on the same water, just different boats. Again, we don't have to understand each other's viewpoint, but we need to accept it.

As a host family blending a new person into whatever your family's demographic is can be difficult. As in the case with this boy. In his culture, being the only male heir entitled him to certain privileges. While with us his status changed dramatically. I have been known to speak that new age faucet of "all kids equal." For me, that's a lie! I don't raise my kids equally at all. I have a standard, but I am also OK with how each of them uniquely reaches that standard. I encourage them all where they are - not where I want them to be! Regardless of their individual needs or directions, we all do equal shares of housework. We have the freedoms, the education, and the ability to raise our kids the same or we can raise them differently! His family raised him differently than his sisters and differently than I would have. That doesn't present a negative obstacle, it presents an opportunity for my acceptance of him and for him to accept me. I consider myself gifted an unreturnable gift every time I get to see another way.

Encroaching the mid-way point some discouraging realizations had to be made. While this young man was doing well with school, socializing outside of school, and peacefully existing in our home, no family bonds were being made. Cultural acceptance can really damage an exchange year. More so it can truly damage peace. He was physically here but nowhere near willing to accept our family dynamic was tolerable. I was raised in the Midwest, core values, country music, hard work, garden hose drinking, middle class, and equal rights. I think most families settle into routines that work but most I know can alter their normal and adjust on the fly. To this boy, based on his culture and personal family life, my role as a mother was to tend to the males of the family. Additionally, my daughters should fall into place with me tending to the men. This simply isn't our way. I usually cook dinner, but my husband can handle it when needed. Standing strong as a host family when our dynamic was insulted was difficult, but our job isn't to change our routines to make him feel at home. Our job is to provide an American experience not duplicate here in the USA what he is used to back at home.

The battle was silent the rest of the year. He did his thing and stayed an entire exchange here in America, but he never experienced being part of an American family. He didn't join us for weddings, birthday parties, and a few other culturally enriching activities. I would ask him why and he would answer he simply wasn't interested in "things like that." His sister even messaged me at one point to encourage me to look after him better, make him feel comfortable, and cook more meat. We had different views on my role as a mom.

The second trip to the airport had tears. Tears for the experience as a host family we didn't get and tears for the boy who refused to accept cultural differences. I haven't exchanged more than a handful of sentences with him since he returned home. Accepting that what I had to give wasn't enough is hard. It's not a failure, it's just another lesson. Kind Growth happens in many ways.

What did I get out of this exchange then?

I got me! My 9th FES taught me not to change according to someone else's picture of culture. Here the way we live, the meals we cook, our customs, achievements, the interactions, and life we make are our culture. A culture formed from heritage and from personal choices. Any exchange student coming here should be ready to embrace the differences, that's the point of the exchange. As a host mom it was difficult to be compared and be found less than adequate. However, it was still valuable learning. Exchange doesn't only teach differences in culture it explores how every culture is vastly diverse, often leaving confusion. It leaves pockets of information about a person, and their home country. It is not a study of their entire country's culture, just theirs.

These kids are rockstars - even the ones who don't like me! They literally are on show the moment they step off the plane and the fact he felt comfortable enough to dislike me is huge! The job as a host family is to welcome them and become a FAMILY! There isn't a magic potion going to make that happen. Any mountain you attempt to climb there is a reality that you might not reach the top and that's ok, make the climb anyway! Some personalities will blend, others will break - that isn't a result of cultural differences or personality differences - that's people! Each exchange students, and their host families, path to understanding and acceptance of people is organic and vital.

So, yeah, I got me! I learned to love my culture for forging this path so I can live this FES life. I also got a bonus personal upfront understanding of why the topics of border patrol and illegal immigration tend to be front line on Presidential agendas and debates. If you have never been discriminated against it's difficult to understand the term. If you have lived a year in your own home, with a person who dislikes you just because you aren't like him, who discriminates in his treatment of you, all because you made yourself vulnerable so he could experience something new. Hosting can go so wonderfully, and it can take a sharp left turn and change epically.

I love to travel and do as often as I can and when I enter foreign countries, I follow their culture. Respect for each other is critical for acceptance. I may not always love those presidential debates and various political agendas, but I respect in their own ways they are trying to protect our homes, their homes, all of our homes from someone coming in and making us feel less than in our own culture. We are not wrong to have opinions. We are only wrong when we allow our opinion to become an agenda. When we use slander to prove our side. When we allow anything but the truth, lead the opinion. Love yourself and the culture you call home, don't apologize to be you! Have your opinions but love the diversity in each other. People all share differently, accepting that is like a needed magical potion.

My 9th FES taught me confidence. Confidence to love my home. If you really examine it, America is really a melting pot of culture, diversity, religion, and so much more. When someone is eager to point out the American Way flaws, they naturally have 3 fingers pointing right back at them. There is no blame or shame in confidently loving your home!

While our paths may have only crossed briefly, I still found growth and I hope he did too! I hope he found ways to remember what he liked here.

Chapter 10

Italy

2016

Baby FES!

To any one of us who have experienced loss, we know all too well how easy it is to close off and keep people at a safe distance. Whatever diagnosis and justification we use it boils down to emotional fear. Each time my international kids return home, there is an emotional shift every darn time. I had learned to keep them close, but not too close, out of fear of repeating that person I was when I sent my first FES home. I had built limits even I wasn't fully aware of. I truly believe people cross paths for multiple reasons. Every once in a while, we are gifted with someone who will destroy every limit, every wall we have built around ourselves. A person who reminds us to look past the package or wrapping and connect to the inside of each other. And most importantly - to quit being afraid of hurt. The more it hurts - the more I learn!

For me, it's my baby FES. Loving him is simply the only option he would allow!

This kid refused to let me stay safe and emotionally unaffected. I teased him often about being the "baby", little does he know how much that title is filled with emotion! How powerful that title really is! Similar to my youngest child where I hold the moments stronger, I cherish the time longer, I feel something unique at the closure of these "last times" with her. My Italian FES demanded me to open up and let it happen, to feel the moments completely. Love can build a bridge, and he didn't just make me walk the bridge, he made me grow emotionally while I did it! That's what these kids do every time you open your home and host, they change something in you. My baby FES continues to help me feel more, hold on longer, and just let it happen!

Now, if I could just get him to appreciate Twilight!

My baby FES!!!!!! He was the tenth exchange student! This is not something I had ever thought was possible when we welcomed our first Norwegian son. We have had a little bit of everything by this time, various cultures, religions, families, financial disparities and attitudes. I have learned so much about myself! My family has learned so much about each other! The family motto of "Different is Different NOT Wrong" has become our culture. I can honestly look back at that very first airport trip and accept I was a naive idiot and feel good about the fact that I changed. It wasn't always easy for any member of my family but together we did it. Sometimes it takes years to find true growth.

Now, it's time for one last FES! I am determined that ten is more than enough FES for one mama! This Italian boy is in for it too, because I plan to love the crap out of him. He better just accept he is going to be a classic spoiled rotten baby FES!!!!

Here's what I got for setting an expectation (again) on my FES! I never did get a chance to spoil him because he spoiled me! He was kind and genuine and his smile was so addicting. He would talk for hours about his family. His mom made amazing meals and he missed those while he stayed here. I am a firm believer in "if it's opened at home, then it's homemade." I do cook, but it's not my happy place.

This FES was incredibly dedicated to basketball. He was thoughtful and purposeful in his actions. He charmed almost everyone into liking him. He probably did a few things he shouldn't have. He experienced so much because he was willing to embrace it all! It's amazing how much as a host family you will be willing to do just because you hear words like "thank you" from you FES! He motivated me to open up. Every morning I had the urge to just hug him! Good thing he was on the same page and enjoyed the affection. He loved to show his emotions any way possible!

Note: physical touch with FES can be a balancing act. Not all cultures appreciate touch, other cultures demand physical connection. I always watch for the silent cues and try to find the balance between what I want and what our FES is comfortable with. Most exchange programs told me to avoid touch.

Baby FES was so easy going. A true laid-back personality. He seemed to have, according to him, a solution to any situation.

Example: he packed four pairs of underwear for his exchange! Only four pairs for the full year! I do laundry daily but with sports no way would four pairs get it done. My solution was to go shopping to purchase a few more. His solution was he would wear his host brothers and save the money!! To him the problem was solved. I am all for sharing but I drew the line at underwear. Years later he and I had a conversation about the underwear he purchased here in America. He said, "I had to adapt to American underwear, one of the most uncomfortable situations I encountered."

Having a son, the same age as FES was double sided. On the one hand, the friendship formed was rock solid. Their shared friendships flowed easily. The parties I am sure were fun! The schoolwork presented little challenge. The bond the two boys had was unique, and strongly formed from the first few weeks. On the other side that bond would be tested, and it was the strongest display of character and kind growth. Experiencing it with them and watching them navigate the trials for themselves and for each other.

I am just going to get the story over with first: This story isn't about the storm so please don't get lost in the details. Its about the mountain these boys climbed!

Basketball was a huge passion to each of them. Each boy started the season the same and eventually had two very different results. Our school superintendent went so far as to call one of them a bigoted racist. The varsity coach would publicly humiliate them both for vastly different reasons. Both of their futures are forever changed by those in charge! The staff in general closed blind eyes. It SUCKED! I am still shocked when I think back to that group of adults who chose to test two teenagers. How the adults zeroed in with their magnifying glasses. Shocked because of all the ways the boys could have reacted and didn't. Anger was felt but not what led to their responses. There were many, many tears from both boys and me. Huge up all night chats. Of course, a period of frustration happened but it wasn't all consuming anger. There were moments when we weren't exactly sure what was "the right way" to handle the various situations that came up that basketball season. Remaining stoic in the face of so much emotion challenged us all.

Each of these boys gifted me with a front row seat to watch how they as 17 years old boys would be tested to show courage in the face of pain and adversity! They were frustratingly tested, and they both kicked that test's ass! The measure of a man's character isn't what others see; it's how he controls himself when others don't see. Each of them in their own way worked through it.

Both of them accepted the life lessons and chose to be quietly courageous. They mastered the life skill of not needing to voice your pain (wanting too but not needing too, there is a difference). They accepted that choices have consequences even if it wasn't your choice. They also learned that not all things are fair. Phew, the bad part is over!

Now, the good stuff! Fast forward a year later, those two boys played basketball together again in Italy. A few more years later - they both watched their sister play college ball - one from Italy, one here in the USA.....thank you technology! Both boys found ways to continue basketball without the encouragement of their home school. I imagine, or hope, the adults involved can also look back and acknowledge growth was needed from all sides. Today those boys still have a rock-solid foundation inspired by true friendship and family. The noise from that basketball season didn't break them, it taught them to depend on themselves, each other, and not someone with a name plate on a desk.

This story was important to share because for me, dealing with home schools has been varied. Every principal and guidance counselor has been solid and steady. Every athletic director has allowed some variations so exchange students could become part of teams. Most teachers have been supportive and encouraging while so incredibly understanding of the language and culture barriers. Concurrently, there were also many coaches who didn't want exchange students here. Many teachers saw exchange students as an interruption. In all my experience, never once did any faculty step up in support of my exchange students when conflict happened. If they did, I was never aware.

What I was made to see was superintendents and school boards all easily passed the responsibility onto others. While it's not the home school's job to advocate for FES, most negative situations that came about were typically a misunderstanding from language or culture. I learned quickly that home schools will welcome my FES, but I will have to be the one to advocate for them.

The home schools that allow these exchange students to come are overall remarkable and generous. My point is that schools are still run by humans, and we all have choices to make in every situation. As a host family sometimes, you won't blend with your FES and sometimes your home school won't blend either. I do feel this situation was the only time I felt my exchange student was treated unfairly by a school system. It is important to know that you may need to advocate for your FES, but I had ten exchange students before I had to!

This situation presented so many opportunities to grow and learn. I called out the comment about racism particularly because it made me as a parent do some hard searching. We are the FES family, surely members of the community couldn't possibly label any of us as bigoted racists? Our FES is from Italy, it's not Switzerland, but still, there's a relatively genuine peaceful relationship between Americans and Italians. Name calling is always hurtful, and partial conversations heard out of context can also be damaging. What I learned after all the dust settled is no one could really answer why the nasty term "bigoted racist" was used.

Bottom line, international learning comes with a cost. I have had community members attack my FES. I have had our FES not like me or not like my family. I have had community parents not allow their kids to be involved with my biological kids because of my FES. I have had school leaders come after our home with figurative torches on fire. All this because there is no way you will ever find an entire community that will support what you're trying to do. Not all people are made for kind growth. Not all people want it. If international acceptance isn't on their agenda, they will do what they can to shut you up, and they will attack the vulnerable. If what you want is acceptance like I did, then start practicing your stiff upper lip now cause you're going to need it!

Having a lifetime of international learning allows you to accept things with a worldly view and that worldly view often scares small town America.

Different is Different NOT Wrong.

Bigotry equals intolerance.
Racism equals prejudice.
Having the ability to knowledgeably talk, and yes even laugh, about differences isn't intolerance: its acceptance.
Having the ability to dedicatedly discuss differences doesn't mean prejudice: its intelligence.
I can't change the opinions of others, but I can say here in our home we practice intelligent acceptance!

Baby FES may have been able to display triumphant courage in the face of truly unfair adversity, but he felt it. I was humbled as a host mom that he was comfortable enough with me to share it. The memories of how some adults treated him here will fade and that's encouraging. It's a shame that this amazing small town will forever be marred by the actions of a few. All these figure heads, who accepted the responsibility to be ambassadors, dropped the ball. Luckily, this kid has stronger memories like his very first scrimmage and of the fans cheering his name. He made great friends. His love for us as his host family masked the noise.

Our family connection was never an issue. He just blended with us very naturally. There were even days he took charge. Like the freezing cold day when I got a frightened phone call from our oldest daughter. She was screaming into the phone, saying a tree was in her car. As I am throwing on shoes to head to help her, FES hears her cries. He never hesitated when he heard her over the phone, that was his sister, and he was going to help! I tried to talk him out of it because I had no idea what I would find when I arrived at the accident scene. He had told me to "shut up" because he was going, like it or not!

Her accident was not far from home, so we found her quick enough. She was understandably shaken but she would be fine. The car was a total loss. She had been on her way home from school so there were books and papers everywhere. Her coat was not accessible. The amazing family whose tree she'd damaged took her inside their home to keep her warm and try to comfort her until we arrived. We do have amazing people in our town! Amazing! When we are scared and emotional, there are always people who will help you handle the stress. If this book ever reaches the hands of that amazing couple - thank you!

I handled the police, wrecker, and business stuff. Once our daughter seemed calm enough to walk her to my car to take her home, I did. I had forgotten all about our FES! This whole time he had been outside in freezing weather, collecting her things, transferring what he could into my car. Seeing us walk out, he ran over and checked in with her immediately, made sure I had her in the warm car, then proceeded to help me clean the mess and assist with the final details for the tow truck driver. The officer, finishing the paperwork, looked at our FES and said, "You need to get inside son!" In all that was happening I had not looked at what FES was wearing. Our FES literally was in shorts and a t-shirt (I think he had on shoes). The officer noticed how cold FES was and wanted FES to get warmed up! FES just loved us like that, it didn't matter if he was seconds away from frostbite, he was all in! From the moment he heard her over the phone he just took charge! I am not sure anything will ever compare to the kindest love I received, my entire family received, from baby FES!

Baby Fes has so many endearing qualities. He has a serious sweet tooth and requires daily "biscuits" or cookies. He was always quick to let me know how much he enjoyed my homemade treats. My rule is if you open it in the home, it's homemade, so yes, Oreos do count! The simple kindness of his appreciation brought me daily smiles. He was always willing to chat while he smashed down his junk food as well.

He wore the same shirts over and over, and boy did I get tired of washing them, but I also learned it's not the packaging that made him so unique. In fact, those darn worn-out shirts are now framed in my barn, holes and all! It was difficult to part with them when he packed to return home because as always FES collects quite a trinket and treasure pile while here, and often a few sacrifices must be made to fit the luggage when returning home. To this day I am glad those shirts got left behind, because I can see them every day and remember the lesson, I learned with baby FES: it's not the package that matters.

He was able to go watch NBA games which was obviously a dream of his. Being able to say you helped someone with their dream, that's heavy stuff! That's FES life at its finest! We took him to comedy shows, which was a bad idea, but there was some amazing frozen ice, so we redeemed that mistake. He also laced up his boots, grabbed a shovel and got dirty helping us build a new recreation barn. No, FES are not free labor! FES do come, however, wanting to be part of your family so LET them work if the family is working! Teaching a FES life skills like trench digging isn't just used in America, every country has sewage lines of sorts! Letting FES hammer nails while framing walls gave him a great life skill! He went to school dances, lock-ins, sporting events, trampoline parks, coached powder puff football, and he embraced it ALL. He even had a role in the high school musical.

He attended family dinners, carved the turkey, supported crazy fighting gift traditions. At Christmas as a tradition, I will literally throw random presents in the air and the kids run, jump, climb, even brawl over getting the present they like best! It's just part of our crazy fun and he participated like it was a normal activity! He went to museums, zoos, and light adventures. He even held babies! He took road trips to check out universities to support his brother. Heck, he teared up over a stupid Oklahoma Thunder poster for Christmas. It didn't matter what he did or where we went, he was thankful, and he expressed it with words and actions. That's how he wore me down and softened my heart! The first 6 weeks FES are often perfect, and on their best behavior. After that their "normal" starts to show. My baby FES's normal just got better and better! He never missed opportunities to make all of us feel special. Some might say it's an Italian thing, I say it's a Baby FES thing!

By special I mean he just kept doing things like getting an in-school suspension for climbing through the ceiling tiles to reach the weight room one day before senior trip!!!! Or joining a group of kids on the school roof, because it seemed like a fun time! It took me 10 FES, but I finally had one willing to spice things up a little! He was willing to accept the consequences of his actions. Of course, the same people with name plates on their desks tried to punish some boys with graduation, others with suspensions, and yet others with detention! I had my FES and my biological son both involved - of course I did! I received two phone calls from two different name plates with two different punishments! This time I was not quiet. It's absurd to have the same crime punished in different ways! My point: The name plates got to see me hurt the first time with the basketball fiasco, and this time they got mama FES bear fighting back! FES are worth every battle you must have. It's just another reality of hosting. That name plate I still see from time to time and seeing him always makes me reflect. He lost so much by not accepting the changes happening. I am not angry at the nameplate or even disappointed, just grateful that baby FES taught me how to love through it all!

Baby FES wore a robe to and from the shower. It was unique to me because of the fabric. Almost terry cloth like. Why does this matter? Because the little memories matter too! Sometimes I can still see him in the hallway in that robe. We do not need a big event to realize the value others have in our life - we only need a robe! Subsequently, he later sent robes for my younger kids too!

An opportunity presented itself for baby FES to go to Florida on spring break with some friends. I am NOW a firm advocate for exploration, travel, and adventure (10 FES will do that to you). I knew he would have some crazy fun! His parents approved and off he went. I think it really hit me that week: I had let every wall down and he was forever going to be my baby! I also realized letting this boy leave at the end of the exchange was going to be bad, bad! Kind Growth hit again.

Baby FES reminded me to love! He taught me to remember the little things. He showed me how to appreciate the redundancy of mundane things. He taught me that compliments are given because someone wants to make you smile so smile, damn it! People listen because they are interested - don't shy away from the attention. Say thank you! Spending quality time with someone doesn't have to have an agenda. We all build invisible barriers we don't need when we believe people have agendas. He also reinforced lessons already taught by former FES, such as I don't have to be right!

Love loves even when I or someone else is wrong.

I don't have to win.

When I attack the situation, I will win some and I will lose some. When I attack the person, I will lose every time. Love those close to me even in the midst of a failure - it's the best win I will ever accomplish!

A dear friend once said: "I love when people talk bad about me, it means they are leaving someone else alone."

Baby FES took his second trip to the airport and my face leaked a bit. It was incredibly difficult to let his light walk through security away from my family and I. I knew our families would stay connected; baby FES wouldn't allow any difference.

The story continues, as we found our time with baby FES was not finished! Our second son headed across the pond to spend the majority of that same summer in Italy with baby FES and his family! Yes, at 17 we simply put our son on a plane to Europe to travel through several countries. That's what a FES life did to me, I learned to release my control, my helicopter parenting, and let my own kid fly! What a difference from Rookie FES to Baby FES! I have gone from fat and lazy to educated and strong! I no longer say, "what if?" All the what ifs, the when's, and the why's are wasted energy. I now say "even if" because even if kindness sucks and the growth hurts, I am learning every day!

Years later, when our first grandchild was born baby FES was back for the entire summer. He wanted to be here because apparently Italian Uncles are the best! I don't know about Italian Uncles, but I KNOW Baby FES is the best! An awesome additional fact is that during that same summer we also welcomed our 12th FES. Baby FES and number 12 got to meet. Which led to another first, having two of my FES meet each other!

As I ventured through writing this book, baby FES has been my hardest to write about. I get about a paragraph in and tear up! As I said before this kid just pulled at my heart. So, I stop and text him and he always responds. An ocean apart and he just always seems to know when I need a "baby FES" chat. He likes to Facetime, and it's so good but so HARD! His voice is equivalent to a heart punch every time. He will sometimes leave voice messages and I will listen to them on repeat. Warning - for those considering hosting - know that some kids will melt your heart and you will never be the same after!!

Chapter 11

Brazil

2018

Obviously, Baby FES did not end up being the last one! Our son was a senior in 2018 and we usually say no FES during senior year. However, that plan didn't work this time around. We did however require our son to get his "college plan" in place before we hosted.

That's how we ended up with our official first half year FES! We have had lots of full year FES, a couple of squatter FESs, an extra short-term FES, exploring FES, we might as well add a half year student to the ever-growing list. The joy of cultural learning comes in so many forms and timelines. Don't dismiss an idea or opportunity because it doesn't fit Plan A, embrace each opportunity because opportunity rarely comes at convenient moments.

Why now? We had closed the chapter of FES life with baby Fes, or so we thought. How many times can you ask your family to repeat kind growth and be willing for the stretching that comes with that growth? I have learned my younger kids simply knew no other life. Having a FES to learn with and learn from was as essential to them as regular high school friends and biological siblings. I have found living a FES life does become a strong part of your identity. Acceptance becomes almost an addiction. You come to crave the lows of hosting almost as much as the highs because of who you become through each trial! During this time, we had a visit by our Azerbaijan son. Whenever the relationships continue past the initial experience of the exchange year, you know you're doing something good. There is a place in my heart that never wants to stop meeting new people!!! Being kind can suck and growing hurts, but what's left after the storm is what lifetime dreams are made of!

Another thing happens while living a FES life. Your children will learn to see people differently. That's the vocalized goal when you start but the growth can hurt a bit. I especially saw this happen with my younger ones who have literally grown up living a FES life. Their acceptance isn't shared with their friend groups. The freedom to travel, explore, and accept change hasn't been accepted by peers the same way. Keeping close friends is a balancing act. Learning that it's ok to be you is harder than it looks. It can be hard to understand why at seventeen you can travel across Europe alone, yet your friends need chaperones to go to Chicago. Knowing your parents do not stand in your way of drinking, sex, or so many other culturally taboo topics, yet your friends hide their birth control.

It was time to switch it up a little. Let's be real, I love coffee and I needed to try some authentic Brazilian coffee! My knowledge of Brazil was minimal apart from the 2016 Olympic highlights and I decided that needed to change. There was a girl here in our town a few years back from Brazil, she was from right outside the capital of Brazil, and she loved city life. She didn't last long here as it is not very common to have maids and servants in the midwest. She was a sweet girl, but she just wasn't ready to accept so much difference so quickly. This FES we were looking at receiving was also from Brazil but unlike the other FES from Brazil, his family's business was farming. I was very curious about what a "farmer" looked like outside of the midwest. I was cautious to compare our new FES to the other Brazilian experience as I was sure they would have their differences.

So, we took that trip to the airport again. Seriously, if we got miles for airport stops, not just flights, we would have been set for future travel! There were several things we forgot to consider when we picked our Brazilian FES in January and welcomed him to the midwest. First, he was perfect and just so darn sweet at the initial meeting. Then we walk outside, and he can see his breath in the cold air for the first time in his life. He stops mid step as he watches the air and just laughs. I love the season changes in the midwest, but I have never stopped to watch my breath in arctic cold weather. Now, every time it's so cold my boogers freeze, I smile at my first memories of our Brazil FES! Experiencing exchange students from other climates made me remember to appreciate the seasons I often take for granted!

It is easy to be kind when your goal is selfish. I am no exception to that theory. My intent isn't to use these kids to better myself. Just because it's not my intent, doesn't change the fact it happens just the same. I am awed over and over at the differences in these FES's personalities, not just the differences in their countries, cultures, and religions, certainly those all play a part in their development as well. Just like each of my own children are different, each one of these students have their own individual identity and unique personality.

Our Brazilian boy had a smile that went on for days. He was quick to give his undivided attention. He was eager to become part of our family. He loved to talk about his family and share their pictures with us. One picture that stuck out to me was the one he showed us of him on his family farm. I found out his farm was actually a few hours away from his home. His dad traveled there weekly and stayed at the farm. Our Brazilian boy wanted to follow his dad's footsteps and become a farmer. I often take for granted that my husband is home with me every night. How many enjoy the comforts of everyday physical touch? That doesn't mean anything is lacking if you aren't together daily, but it certainly doesn't make things easy. My husband traveled for work for years and now is home daily. I would take a daily partner over a traveling partner every time. I had forgotten those days when I had to single mom it and unplug my own toilets, but this boy's stories brought those days to my remembrance again.

Gun control can cause cities to divide, friends become foe, and families to unite. It's a powerful argument on each side of the debate here in the USA. Our exchange student didn't join the debate; he simply joined discussions on the differences between our countries. My husband is an avid hunter and owns many guns. He spends weeks in the forest and various properties, donating the meat he hunts to families in need, and enjoying guys' trips. He loves the comforts of nature, the smells, the cold, all of it. I had never thought to worry or fear for his safety while he was out because he was always armed. While he enjoys his hobby, he has the freedom to carry the gun that yes is purposed for the hunt but also protects him should he be out in the forest and become the hunted! Accidents can happen anywhere, and wildlife can be unpredictable. We found out gun laws are very different in Brazil. We learned while our Brazilian's family is out working their properties for their livelihood, they cannot carry a gun to protect themselves should their natural wildlife attack them. I don't claim to understand all the debate, but I do know I am personally thankful my husband has a gun while hunting.

Back to the picture Brazil FES showed me: It is just a basic landscape photo taken from inside the vehicle down at their farm. It's a gorgeous landscape. Brazil has a lot of beautiful land.   I was focusing on the details of the picture when I noticed a black cat very close to their vehicle.

"Is that a panther?!" came out of my mouth.

FES laughed at my reaction, and then proceeded with a discussion of the big cats in his area. This was amazing to me. In my hometown, we get newspaper articles if too many coyotes are spotted. It's a big deal to have bigger wild animals around here aside from deer. Here he has a picture with a panther outside his vehicle and it was no big deal. A Panther!

Here he is with his dad in a country that's always warm, on a farm miles away from their family, with large wildcats beside their car and no guns! I asked him how they would defend themselves if a cat attacked. He responded diplomatically and simply said, "If you give them space, they usually leave you alone."

It was just his way. My mind stayed stuck on the word "usually". So, what happens on an unusual day? I guess I will have to visit Brazil someday to find out if I have the courage!

Every time I watch a city divided over debatable topics, each time I see a friendship ruined over strong opinions, and every darn time I see families shatter over the lack of acceptance I remember this kid. Whether we are pro-gun control/against it, I have accepted that we all offer valuable points of view. Tolerance and Acceptance are two uniquely different yet acutely similar actions. We need to practice them both!

Some other things this FES taught me was to stop complaining about the season changes and appreciate their magic, to touch daily if you can, and support those with family far away who don't have that luxury. I learned to love what "usually" happens. An "unusual" day will eventually come and in the end, it probably won't matter what side of any debate you were on.

School and friends were gravy for this kid. Adults, peers, young and old people alike appreciated his open candor and his interest in the United States. On road trips he would make us stop so he could get out and touch the soil. Our variety of soil, clay, muds, and different dirt was interesting to him. He took endless pictures of silos, tractors, farm equipment, and good old-fashioned dirt. His passion for country living was enamored by us all. He researched our farm GPS devices and ultimately even purchased some digital farming devices for himself. I don't think I have ever met a kid more excited to join the family business than him. I Have watched children take over various family businesses out of obligation or expectation, but this kid wanted to be with his dad on the farm!

I think as American families we get so busy chasing the dream we forget to teach the dream. I often have forgotten to check the soil I am planting my roots in. This wonderful kid reminded me to teach my kids about how they plant their roots. It's not just about where the roots are planted but how they are planted.

This 11th exchange student reminded me that my very own culture is about to be on the endangered species list if I don't find ways to accept everyone! I must practice tolerance in situations I oppose and continue to grow in acceptance. I wear a lot of different hats on any given day but the most important is that of Coach (ironic because sports and I don't speak the same language). I must never stop learning and I must never stop encouraging the same of others. The American dream isn't a race, it's a repetitive lesson. Once I, or anyone for that matter, stops learning we lose the vision of the basic dream that the Declaration of Independence spoke of and our country was made of.

Most exchange students arrive with a few gifts for the family. Often, they are themed around their hometown or home country. Our Brazilian FES' grandma made some towels for us which I loved. I had never owned monogrammed or personalized bathroom towels at that point. Now the original ones she made have worn out, but I always keep those personal hand towels in the bathrooms and cherish the memories from them. It was a way of keeping Brazil here even when our FES exchange was over. Over the years, his grandma has sent us many gift packages full of personalized towels and blankets for new babies. The relationships with FES's extended families is one so unique and mysterious. We had never met her, yet she wanted to thank us and continues to show us that gratefulness to this day. Genuine kindness from a stranger shows how powerful connection to families all over the world can be.

What did I learn from number 11 FES? I learned to remember to appreciate the little things, to remember to breathe in the cold weather and get mud on my shoes. I learned to remember to appreciate the season changes and to be in the moment.   All these things became physically and metaphorically valuable parts of my identity.

Chapter 12

Taiwan

2018

Can they come any sweeter?

Our baby girl is a sophomore, and this will be the first time she takes on the responsibility of an exchange student! Our baby is a focus driven girl. She often gets sucked into the tunnel of reaching the goal that she forgets to relax. This also does not make her an ideal host sister from strictly the "hosting" perspective. As an ambassador for our country, she is by far a brilliant example for others to watch. As a mom, I must remind her often to adjust her sails because she fights strongly to keep things under control! You can't control life with FES!

Picking out an exchange student to match that intensity is impossible. No data sheet on any exchange student is going to truly describe their character. After many back and forth discussions we decided to select a girl. There were lots of logical reasons such as if they are on the same teams and same schedule at school, transportation would be easier. As far as the bedroom situation we like our exchange students to share a room because it causes them to communicate and not retreat. Years of experience at this point also told us we wanted a quiet personality. Again, no data sheet can tell me this. We would have to meet her to learn her traits and personality. Our search began and we took our time.

This girl took the longest for us to pick out and was the most detailed selection we personally have ever had in our experience with FES. We temporarily got our microscopes back out to read through bios with detailed goggles on. Putting two teenage girls in the same room involved a lot more consideration than boys. In my experience raising teenagers and young adults I have learned some basic truths. Not all the boys that have lived here have liked each other or even got along. For example, my oldest son and Rookie FES couldn't stand each other.

Basic truths I have learned about boys: They figuratively piss on trees to mark their territory and their claim. Rules of engagement demand another male to respect this territory. If a territory or claim is breached a physical altercation often occurs followed by an immediate armistice.

 Basic truth: Girls DO NOT follow the same Geneva Convention.

I can say with embarrassment I shielded away from Asian cultures. I would keep my selection filters on Europe or South America and males because I convinced myself those cultures blended best here and chose boys because I appreciated the laws of war! With my daughter helping me choose this time, I had already accepted I was removing the male filter. I might as well stop lying to myself saying I was accepting international learning as I was only planning to accept vetted parts! It took the strongest amount of courage for me to clear those filters and find this new student. I cleared the filters and there she was. She was the top girl!   Number twelve and it was fully decided, she was going to be a girl! There she was smiling at my family, silently demanding that I pay attention to her through her bio picture.

The summer before she arrived was jam packed with FES life! From June until August our extra bedrooms were full, overflowing to the point we were even pulling out air mattresses to house everyone! Sadly, still just one bathroom but we had learned to rock the 5-minute shower!

May:
Our youngest son had just graduated High School in May. We had a huge graduation party to get through, and then off to the airport to send our Brazilian boy home.

June: We opened our home again to our Rookie FES and his family. Yes, he came back again and this time he brought the whole family!!! Together our families traveled some of the USA and spent a week on the beach watching the Atlantic Ocean roll in. Our international family time saga continued! Oceans and years apart, yet still so many of my international kids are very much part of my family. Our Norwegian friends left after a couple weeks. It is always so hard to say, "until next time".

July: We welcome our Italian son who showed up with a friend. The Italian boys and our son hopped in the car and went to Niagara Falls, Fenway Park, Times Square, Washington DC, and stood next to Rocky at the Philadelphia Museum of Art! If that wasn't enough excitement for a summer, we welcomed our first grandchild in July.

August: FES girl's arrival. When her flight was scheduled in August, our Italian son was still here. For the first time EVER two of our exchange children would meet each other. Pinch me please! I have no idea what I did to deserve this life! My American home in those four months was home to Brazil, Norway, Italy, and Taiwan! We had the world in our home.

She's here. She smiled nonstop. She loved pictures and held up the peace sign with her fingers. She is soft spoken and so intelligent. Enrolling in school is anxiety filled for her because academic excellence is vital. Her course selection is meticulous. She eventually decides, begins her classes, and finds a flow easily. Local kids are typically very engaging with new students, so she quickly makes some friends. Homecoming lands in the fall, and she scandalously has her nails painted for the first time. It was scandalous to her, but beautiful to me! She wore a delicate dress and all but brought me to tears in her wonder of experiencing an American Homecoming. It was official, no matter the differences that I thought my filters protected me from, I was totally in love with this girl!

A couple months later she came home from school in tears! One of my biggest worries about girls apart from the Geneva Convention was their emotions. I am not a very gifted mom when it comes to being delicate about emotions. Basic rule: teenage emotions are scary as crap! "I can do this" became my repeated mantra. "I suck at this" became the reality of my mantra! She came home in tears because she sat at her lunch table, answering questions from kids about her home country. I want to stop right here and point out that teenagers sitting around chatting about cultural differences is a big part of what this FES experience is all about!!!

Learning in a boarding school environment with little social interaction and vast amounts of educational requirements - the American High School experience was opposite anything she had ever known. Talking at the lunch table was new to her. Choosing seats, meal options, even simple things like slouching were new. The girls here wanted to know about her lunch or school schedule, and she shared her typical day with them. She explained to this group at her table that at her school everyone walked through the line, they were given a meal, they sat as ordered, no speaking, both feet on the floor, facing forward, the meal was timed, and you returned to class. That was her normal. As she explained this routine several of the girls here laughed at her and said they would never attend a school like that.

Our FES was crushed at the thought of others not accepting her way of life and worse, not liking it. Coming from a culture typically very infused with a need to please people and do what is right the rejection hurt her in a variety of ways. Now, don't go hating on the mean girls, acceptance takes a while for us all, which is why I decided to write this book in the first place!!! So here I sat trying to be motherly to this sweet emotionally upset Taiwanese girl. As far as mean girls go to me this was pretty mild. To my sweet Asian FES these girls were brutal. Then, I had an aha moment! I explained to my FES that she came here wanting to explore and learn about America. Honestly, mean girls are very cultural here! She wanted the full experience and having a couple girls go all Regina George on her was classic American High School!

Sadly, the tears became a normal occurrence. This kind girl had never dealt with how crass and brutal others can be. I was lucky enough that she felt comfortable confiding in me. Every time she would address me with another example of how words from others hurt her feelings, I was able to learn a truth I really hadn't even thought was a problem. I had to acknowledge how often I would ignorantly use insensitive language. Teasing people often leaves deep wounds. I also became aware of how those around me used sarcasm to avoid accountability. Kind Growth had struck again. Be accountable for the words you use and the tone you take. Be purposeful in kindness.

It's a pattern here in midwest America when you see someone to ask, "How are you?". I wonder; however, do we care what the response is? Or are we simply attempting to be polite and move on? For me, I have personally made myself more accountable to that question. I also have made myself more accountable to my answer. When I am asked that question, I respond very robotically "Wonderful, Terrific, and Fantastic". The reactions I get often make great conversation! More times than not I get a smile and I like to think maybe I put that smile there! There may be one time when I say it and it will have the effect on someone else the way the card the doctor sent me, or the old man at the reservoir, had on me. Even if it never has some profound effect on anyone, I still want to be intentional with my connection with people. I also have a twisted sense of humor and silently laugh at the acronym WTF.

Mean girl lesson learned; our FES forged ahead. She became a cheerleader! She was scared shitless!!! I really didn't personally know any cheerleaders at the school, but I did know her nemesis mean girl was on the squad. Man, had I cheated myself in past years! Why had I never involved myself more with the cheer program? The cheerleading coaches, the cheer moms, the other girls made this exchange a full experience for our girl! They gave her rides, took her out to meals, taught her how to do hair, and invited her into their homes! I won't even get started on the year end banquet because the cheerleading banquet is where it's at! I had had a lot of kids go through my home, yet the "filter" had blocked cheerleaders. Now I was learning about an entire group of some of the best kids ever, mean girl included!

She even survived when we attended her games, and our youngest son would scream out "That's my Asian!!!" Interestingly enough some took offense to that, yet our girl was so proud to be our Asian. Perspective has a funny way of being double sided. When a brother yelled out support for his exchange sister, he yelled it with love and a kindness that encouraged them both. Our Asian loved the attention and adored the title "my Asian" because it made her feel she belonged within our family and yet gave honor to her identity as an Asian. An interaction so special to both of them, torn apart from judgmental observations. Just because someone else viewed it through their beer goggles does not make it wrong. If you know your words are positive and are purposeful, and the receiver receives it that way, then others can kiss it! This fits one of my all time favorite quotes I mentioned earlier and will mention again: "Find out who you are and do it on purpose - Dolly Parton"

We are a FES family, we have lived it, we have the scars from each and every battle, we will not allow culturally uneducated people to lessen the purpose of what we are doing! Be accountable in your words and be accountable to your reaction to words you hear. Anyone can sit back and be offended. It takes a strong person to accept a situation they don't understand. When I say be accountable to the words you use and the tone you take, I mean it. To me, that includes when I hear perceived offensive speech. Before I open my mouth to share my opinion, I evaluate the purpose and intent of whatever I observed. If I don't have all the facts does my observational opinion have merit? I will forever continue to call my sweet girl "My Asian" because she is a piece of Asia forever in my heart!

This girl began her stay with us right after our first grandson was born. She had no experience with small kids or infants. Just like household chores and home projects, most exchange students will blend if you give them opportunities. After a couple months she could handle spit up, dirty diapers, and baby cries all night long. She learned the baby's temperament and had no issues changing diapers or cleaning spit up. We welcomed her to be an aunt and she was graceful and giving. I think she misses that boy now more than she misses the rest of us. Can you imagine the discussion she may have years in the future when she does something with her own child that she learned here in America!   Imprinting something so fundamental is a gift we were able to give each other.

For our son's birthday that year, we got him a new pair of shoes. While he was super excited about the gift she was rather upset. She wanted to know why we would give him such a thing. Such an unusual reaction. She explained that in her country, if you gift someone with shoes, you want them to walk away or go away. Ha! I love this. We continued the conversation and learned how many things in her home country have very symbolic meanings. Like gifting a clock or a watch is considered a very aggressive gift as it means "their time is up."

So, yes, we intentionally purchased many clocks and watches that year for Christmas not because our intentions were negative, but we adored sharing such a private story with her. Also, because after opening we could allow her to share the meaning of the gift in her country. Creating opportunities and moments for culture to be shared!

Like our Venezuelan she also added her love to my charm bracelet. Her family sent thoughtful and creative gifts throughout the year. In my kitchen there is hanging artwork from her. So many visitors ask about what the picture says. I have no idea, I don't read Chinese, but I can pull it off the wall and read the English translation she put on the back! Her handwriting is always there to help me translate.

As the year progressed, she learned to understand the differences in our culture's direct speech. She formed a thick skin to perceived mean girls. She allowed the American way to become part of her. Observing someone make such huge strides toward acceptance was again why she will always be "Our Asian".

Watching her learn from school friends and branch out was so much fun! Exchange students are brave enough to come here, and as a host mom one of my biggest growths was allowing them to fly while they are here. Rookie FES had a host mom scared of the rules and frightened by the unknown. Now I push my international kids to fly. I love when I don't see them for days! Their stories and adventures are happening because they were brave enough to come to the United States and because I grew to be brave enough to let them grow too!

Helicopter parenting is real, it's an emotional rut, it doesn't allow for trust to grow. It took a few years but my laid-back responses to teenage parenting are the direct result of seeing what happens when you let the kids decide for themselves! If I did my job when they were small, then my biological kids have the skills needed to make good decisions! My opinion of curfew is don't have one! Rules - be kind and have a purpose! I am here to guide and direct, not hold the shackles to their steel shoes!

In all complicated simplicity it took me til number twelve FES to learn to clear the filters!

Taking her to the airport was uncomfortable as I had to accept a new reality this time. All that worry I had early on about the Geneva Convention was much like all the worry I had to clean under the stove. It was all in my head!

 As my daughter and my FES made a last stop at Starbucks and we simply shared a few last moments as a trio, I realized my baby girl was truly separating from her international sister! The two had formed, in all their differences, an amazing connection. Kind Growth was not just affecting me, my daughter was learning it too! Yes, Rookie FES touched a little girl in a superhero kind of way. Now, years later, these two sweet girls had formed an intentional relationship and would now be geographically separating. Who would have thought my goal setting, overly serious, sometimes bullheaded baby girl would be uniquely attached to my sweet hearted, sensitive, and emotional Asian?

Again - I will beg. Clear the filters!

Chapter 13

Spain

2019

Our amazing boy from Spain was the first time I considered ending the exchange before the first airport ride.

Yes - you read that right!

Once I got the email information and began the first communications with this boy, I knew we were going to clash. I had no doubt our youngest son would handle him but I wasn't so sure about the rest of the family - or myself.

While everyone in the family participates and forms relationships with our FES, the organization and main communication falls to me. I am the proverbial human resource manager, so all information flows through my office!

He was passionate to prove his side from email one. He also wasn't afraid to place blame outside himself. Fundamentally, no matter how much cultural learning I do and how much I push myself to accept differences I have come to learn a lot of things about myself. One of my most basic truths is accountability. We all have a level of accountability in all things we do. I can like the hardest kid in town if he is accountable for his choices. I think my very first German boy taught me that. He too liked to argue, or more specifically, he liked to be right. Remember, he's the one that made our family adapt the rule that you can argue any topic you want but it has to stand on its own merit. You can not argue your side by putting down others point of view or another person (reference computergate - when I smashed #3 German FES's computer for disrespecting grandma).

So much doubt before we ever even met. I had only had a few emails back and forth. Why were my warning bells sounding so loudly?

Then I had a chat with myself. I do that sometimes; I literally talk out loud my concerns to myself. Sometimes we need to have a conversation with ourselves to get to the bottom of what is really going on. What I decided after my talk with myself is that I was a coward. I was letting a couple of red flags cause me hesitation. International learning comes in all forms, and I was forgetting that.

Were our differences cultural or were they personal? At this point I knew that I KNOW how to screw up being a host mom! I also KNOW how to fix each situation to the best of my ability and move on. Would these obstacles completely block progress, or would they be steppingstones to a better understanding of each other? Obviously, I decided to be brave, accepted the challenge and embraced the potential obstacles as opportunities. This was Kind Growth!

I have already pointed out these kids are rock stars! I brought him home from the airport and dropped him off at soccer practice a couple hours later! He made friends almost instantly! He was a great addition to the team. He was given a nickname just as quickly.

Still jet lagged, he also went on a college visit with his host sister and ended up playing some softball with our older boys all within his first 24 hours here! I have come a long way from the host mom who allowed time for her baby FES to adjust. Now I hold more of a survivalist mentality. I just throw life at them and watch them fight their way through. These kids are hungry, and they learn so much more by feeding themselves. Sorry Rookie FES!

We have a video of this kid, fresh off the plane, exhausted, and putting on a softball mitt for the first time in his life. The reason he ended up playing softball was because our older son's team was short a man and they needed a body! They asked our Spaniard to play, and he said, "Sure, what do you need me to do?" We often forget baseball/softball are not so popular around the world. Our team is the guest team, so we bat first. They bury our Spaniard in the lineup, but he still must bat first inning. No warmup, no stretch, just here's a bat. He had never swung a bat yet managed to go 3 for 4 by the time the game was over. He had no clue how to run bases, or why base coaches screamed at him, or how to catch. Yet by the time the game was over not only was he our team's MVP, the opposing team's entire roster wanted to help him anyway they could. He was willing to make himself vulnerable to be accepted. This was a strong life lesson for me. I was also willing to make myself vulnerable when I wasn't sure what this FES was going to bring to the table.

Softball probably wasn't going to be an option for him to continue but it sure was fun! And to live that day over and over, that is what our beautiful America can look like! People from many towns, welcoming the new kid, encouraging him, laughing with him as he learned the new way, everyone invested in growth!

Soccer, unlike baseball, was a natural sport for him. Our soccer coach took him right under his wing and found a home for him on the team. The soccer team we have here is probably the most open and accepting program I have ever witnessed. Walking him for senior night was a very special moment to me and I think him too. He had found a home here outside of just our family and seeing that experience is truly one of my favorite parts of hosting!

He had no issues academically with classes or assignments. Socially he made so many friends I think he may have struggled a bit keeping up with the fast pace of American teens. He had no issues getting in strange cars or going to strange places. He wasn't a picky eater, so he was comfortable eating anywhere they put a plate in front of him.

Basketball was something he really wanted to explore and improve his skills. He was able to try out and he did make the team. He learned the joys of wins and losses. He was able to ride the all-American school bus and participate in all things team meal related. He was so focused on improving that he spent many additional hours getting shots and conditioning.   He would often get so focused we would have to remind him to interact with us.

He handled the holidays wonderfully. He was respectful of all the gifts he received. He enjoyed our traditions and was very involved with preparations. He cooked us a traditional dish and we learned he makes good food, but also makes tremendous messes in the kitchen.

He drew the attention of the ladies rather quickly. It happens! At this point I accepted it and simply added guidelines to keep everyone honest. Those red flags I talked about earlier would be tested in this area. Our Spaniard was relatively young for an exchange student. The friend group he was making had very liberal opinions and they weren't afraid to use them to their advantage. Don't get your underwear in a twist, I mean liberal opinion in the very basic definition of generally emphasizing the need for the government to solve problems. American laws regarding sex can be tricky in high school with some kids being legal age and others not. American morals can be downright oppressive. Trying to navigate your way through

American High School as an outsider not fully understanding the consequences to verbiage used can be overwhelming. Heck, I have lived here my entire life and still often struggle being politically correct in my verbiage.

He had been to a few parties, and I was saddened by his choices of behavior. He was very drawn to kids that allowed and encouraged him to make poor choices. On the opposite side of that he did have lots of fun! I held him completely accountable to any choice he made. I also understand as an exchange student sometimes your immaturity allows you to accept a herd mentality. I really have no problem with that, but the consequences of an exchange student's actions can be huge.

As a host mom, I have learned I have to balance teaching what I will stand for and what the law will stand for. I have yet to find a way to teach the unwritten moral laws hidden in small towns! Ten months isn't anywhere near long enough for the valuable relationship bond of trust and respect. Any time I tell a kid no, I am the enemy and any time I say yes, I risk allowing them to make life changing choices without a full understanding of the consequences. I also must add the comparison to my own children who have had the time to build the relationship of trust or lack of.

I had already learned with this boy that he behaved rather entitled. He was very quick to argue, and he didn't hold back opinions about his perceived grievance. Teenagers are always moving forward with their maturity and growth. Allowing them the freedom to learn or to fail is a balancing act I think all parents struggle with.

I received a phone call late February that put me in the unique situation of not only needing to advocate and help my exchange student navigate a potential issue, but also another exchange student in the community.
While I do not know what did or didn't go down (and I don't need the details)
I followed the verbiage just fine.
Words were being used that could have extreme legal repercussions.
Words tossed around with intentions of vilifying others.
Words that could potentially permanently alter the course of several teenagers' lives.

After some personal investigation I really felt the situation was completely blown out of proportion. I still had a concern that if overheard by the wrong people the negatives could still create waves as the verbiage used was bad. So, I decided to direct my FES on how to navigate this situation. Every country, state, and community have policies to follow but as I have said before, the fear of breaking a rule or policy often kept me from being a good host mom. In this case I chose to be proactive and hopefully that translated to being a good host mom, but I may never know.

First, I addressed my Spaniard, and we had a very open conversation. I gave some direction to his questions. He confirmed what I already suspected in that the situation had been blown out of proportion.

Second, I made the very difficult call in addressing the other host family regarding their exchange student. My sense of responsibility to protect my exchange student, the actions I took, resulted in hurting a lifetime friend. That's a loss I must carry. I have confidence it was the right action. Having confidence doesn't undo the hurt.

The reality of international learning and Kind Growth has a price. It's the tangled web that's weaved when you manage to deceive. It is important to encourage exchange students to be open about all things because moments may come that they don't understand the ramifications of their actions until lifetime friendships are broken. This has happened with two of our exchange students. Each time the friends looked to their parents to fix the issue. Each time I held my exchange students responsible and expected them to do differently. In advocating to and for my FES, I also learned he wasn't going to take responsibility for his part in the process. Although this situation had been fabricated and multiplied for sensationalism, he still had put himself in a position for the rumors to start. It was a poor choice by him. That part of the issue was no one's fault but his own.

We squeezed in a spring break trip to Florida. A few days of just us allowed a lot of learning about each other to happen. Some of this was wonderful from a cultural point of view. He was able to meet some of our relatives who live there. We were able to watch him show kindness to others. So many wonderful positives came from our trip to Florida.

This kid was fun. He really did reach out to experience new things. He just had an energized personality. He was incredibly social and active. He spent countless days, nights, and weekends with a variety of friends. Really, the only problem I had was he didn't particularly bond with anyone in our house. Yes, we were friends, but we didn't cross that plateau where friends become family. I still feel unsettled about this kid because I think we were almost there, and the potential to break those last few barriers was forming. Florida had really helped him be more observant of us.

Florida had finally launched the relationship...and then COVID happened. Need I say more?

A few short days later our boy was sent home. To one of the worst covid infected areas of Spain. We had four days after we returned from Florida. Four days to create memories and seal the family ties. Perspective is hard when he chooses to spend his last few days with friends instead of with us. Usually, I would say building a relationship with friends is more valuable because the family connections stay strong long after the exchange year. Arguing with him was a futile endeavor. He was so stubborn. I was faced with spending his last few days here arguing with him or accepting his position to value friendships over his host family.

While I know he didn't understand fully, we were not sending him home. The organization made that decision. It was very hard for him to accept, and he let it be known he placed a fair amount of blame on me, which wasn't mine to bear. Nothing about covid was fair! It didn't help that other FES organizations in the community followed other guidelines and they stayed the remainder of the year.

Our organization's decision to send him home was made based on his health and welfare. Health was easy to argue. He wasn't any safer here or returning home. Welfare was another new lesson to all of us and ultimately the lesson that sent him home. How would his welfare recover if something happened to his natural family? If he himself got covid here?

Covid brought us to a world full of people who wanted to be angry at someone. A demand for racial wrongs to be righted. An outcry of political injustice happened here in America. A prince left the confines of working royal life. Millions of people fell in love with the Tiger King for goodness sake! Toilet paper disappeared and face masks showed up. School aged kids learned virtually, and social distancing became the new normal. Black hornets arrived. Add to that a presidential election which promoted slander and division even more. Riots and anger were everywhere.

Building the relationship with this sweet boy from Spain was going to be harder than I thought and is still a work in progress. He looks left, I look right. He says yes and I say no. He is very passionate when he talks, and I have to remember "I don't have to win."

I count any conversation that he doesn't call me an "American" as a win! When he calls me an American it is NOT a compliment.

My time was cut short and as with so many things covid related it simply sucks!

However, I wouldn't change a thing about meeting this boy! He reminded me of all the colors and sides I miss when I only see the confrontation. My heart keeps being moved, bent, shaped, and opened one FES at a time.

I hope to see this boy again. I want to have the conversations that were taken away. The FES life changes so quickly, so we must make every moment count! That was what I learned with FES #13.

Chapter 14

Netherlands

2020

While we all navigate the disruptions of pandemic living, the show must go on! Mental health issues are on the rise, the presidential election process has lost a level of integrity it once had, people have lost so much. If I have learned anything at all as an international parent, it is that if I want to see the change then I better start finding a way to BE the change. I always start with the girl I see in the mirror!

Now, how to navigate positive change during a pandemic?

For me I go to what I know works - acceptance! I accept if you want to stay inside and patiently wait for the storm to pass. I accept if you want to captain the full ship on open water as well. Science is unarguably the light house for us all. Faith will lead some to science and others in different directions. I am keeping my eye on that lighthouse for sure and I am enjoying all this new family time! The house projects completed, the conversations, the acceptance to allow others to do what feels right to them is so powerful. Standing up for myself by keeping my circle small has given me a confidence I lacked. I am not going to carry on about the negative effects of 2020. I am going to be thankful for balance and for the reopening of borders because that means the exchange programs are still a go! Welcome to America. One last time - AND I MEAN IT- ish!

Our daughter was a senior and she wanted a FES. I knew so many things about this senior year would be different. The pandemic had brought her junior year to a screeching halt and this final senior year was looking to be open yet full of "new normal" guidelines. She hadn't decided about university, field of study, or even her general direction. It wasn't the best time to get a FES. For me 2020 was more about focusing on what I could control, not what I couldn't control. Still, I decided to go ahead with her desire for a FES.

The fun part, picking out your FES!!
Was NOT so fun………. The struggle was real with covid restrictions, the dilemmas of which country border was open and when, and not all the new questions had clear understandable solutions. So many delays came for so many various reasons. Some countries have open borders, some don't. Countries that were issuing visas couldn't fly to the USA due to our rules here. Quarantines and flight restrictions are all part of this new normal. Previously, we picked our FES off a letter, trying to match up interests of the FES and our family. Now, we were navigating open borders vs interests.

We struck the proverbial FES lottery!

We picked our girl (yes, we are going to finish with a girl, remember, my filters were now off) and while the pandemic created some wrinkles; she had her visa and was simply waiting for her organization to schedule her flight...and waiting...and waiting...2 weeks later...still waiting...

School starts and we are still waiting for a flight. This is NOT how this is supposed to work! I am getting frustrated because those first few days of school are so rewarding, and I didn't want the FES to miss it! Note if you decide to host, always try to get your student before the start of the school term. It's much better for an exchange student to walk in fresh and new the same as everyone else, to experience life and school.

While searching into the cause of the delay I discover the organization on the Netherlands side is closing, the pandemic created too many financial strains. I also found out the kids and families were going to be notified the following week. Additionally, I learned, once these kids get notified from their home organization, their exchange year is over. The exchange programs, from my experience, work in branches. Our girl's local branch was closing, and the main European branch would eventually absorb it, but that would take time and not happen right away. Time our girl did not have if she was going to come this year. On the United States side our girl was good to come, all the paperwork was dotted, and the t's were crossed. Even the insurance was done.

Researching how she could possibly still come this year, I stumbled across what appeared to be a loophole. Once in the United States it didn't matter if her local organization closed, because her visa had already been approved and the United States had already accepted her. If her local organization officially notifies her, her exchange year is over. BUT if she was already in the states when they attempted to notify her, she could stay. Once here she is fully under the United States program protection. Now, how exactly do I try to communicate that with her parents?

Can you imagine getting an email: "Hi, this is your daughters soon to be host mother. I want you to book a flight for your daughter and send her to me immediately. The organization you hired to handle the exchange from the Netherlands side is going out of business, you and your daughter will be notified next week of the closure, once officially notified all documents are void and your daughter's exchange year is over before it starts. So please just book her a flight, send her to me, and we will get the details figured out retroactively. I assure once she is here, she has full exchange protection and support."

My response would probably have been something like: "Catfish RUN"

Luckily, for all of us her dad also researched everything. He seemed to come up with the same information and he took me at my word that I would get his daughter from the airport. With a small window of time, she was booked, packed, and on a plane. This is when we discover she is in the air without the required paperwork to clear customs. She has the documents, just not on her. So, her parents sent them to me. However, I myself am en route to the airport. I sure hope customs have a personality because we have e-documents, no Netherlands organization, and an exhausted seventeen-year-old girl!

I spoke earlier about advocating for your exchange student. Hosting isn't a place to sit back and observe. A host must act, react, and adjust at all times of the exchange year. Sometimes, like with this situation, you even must advocate before you ever physically look at your FES for the first time. I learned early on that allowing someone to minimize the incredible courage a FES brings to us can't happen. A host must take a walk in their shoes, NOT just their culture shoes or race shoes, but their "I am a person shoes". The road a host walks will change both the life of the FES and the life of the host themselves. It is important to think it through before reducing any person to a singular descriptive word. A good host will advocate for acceptance even if that means advocating for someone they have never actually seen.

Moving on…she is here!

Fabulous number fourteen.
Her English was incredible! The words she did stumble on she asked quickly about and learned. She was tall, blonde, beautiful blue eyes, intelligent, thoughtful, and incredibly shy! We learned she was taking this exchange in America for a year to engage herself. To be patient and find some direction as to what she wants to do next. Imagine any teenager you know being willing to step back for an entire year to evaluate their next step! Do we have American teenagers with that level of patience? Do we as parents have the patience to accept when our child isn't ready for university, but isn't ready for the work force either? I think as a culture we put too much power into the magic age of eighteen. "Growing" with the flow isn't always done in eighteen years. Patience is a concept I needed to

understand and start applying to my life. I would soon discover how valued the lesson of patience would mean to me!

I said she was shy. I wasn't kidding. She could become the proverbial wallpaper and blend in all situations. She was very comfortable in the back seat. We quickly encouraged her to join a fall sport. As with many small towns, extracurricular activities are where important socialization takes place. Just because a kid is brave enough to cross the pond does not mean they are equipped with built in steel armor. She took our advice and joined a team, where she sat away from the group and was genuinely miserable the entire season. Come time for the next sports season, we didn't push. While socialization is part of the exchange - it's only part. Remember the rate of progress isn't as important as understanding the unique personalities all FES (all people) have and accepting that we all adapt and connect differently.

She adjusted to our home as if she always belonged there. She adapted to our routines and behaviors without a single push back. That is rare! While she was adapting, she really wasn't investing herself in this experience. I think a lot of that was because she had contact with her natural family and friends' way too much. So much so that it began to create a barrier between us. Which was frustrating. She wasn't socializing with any friends here, heck, she wasn't even making friends! She adapted to life with us but was perfectly happy to communicate all thoughts and feelings with her invested friends and family from home. It's as if she was here in body, but all other parts were completely back home in the Netherlands.

It was disheartening to think we would finish our exchange life with a kid that really didn't want to invest in us as a family. That said, she also brought to my attention that I needed to stop thinking about me and realize she was struggling to make it all work as well. Watching her I realized, it wasn't so much that she didn't want to invest in us, more like she was already full. She had great parents, great friends, and a great family. Trying to find places for others in an already full life is a difficult task for any of us.

I had to stop having a personal pity party and start trying harder to plant the seeds. If I wanted her to connect - I needed to seize opportunities to show her how valued, she was within our family and how invested I was to find ways to include her. I had to commit to planting the positives and hope for the harvest. I am sure any Olympian will tell you "Sure they wanted the gold" but I am equally positive no Olympian ever regretted getting to compete, and I wanted a spot in her heart! Hasn't the point of all this kind growth been to learn new ways?

Diligently, I went to work seizing opportunities and planting the idea that we could fit into her amazing heart. I also took a good look around me and realized in my life she wasn't the only one I knew struggling to find ways to blend into new families, specifically into my family. Once again FES are teaching me personally applicable life skills! I also have to acknowledge that like my sweet girl from the Netherlands, the partners my children bring into their lives may not have the space for me that I long for now. How brilliant that I get the opportunity to not only watch my children grow up, and find strong partners, but that I also get a lifetime of challenge and growth myself with the new relationships that are added!

197

How can I ever thank my Netherlands girl for helping me see that patience is needed?

Building bridges, planting seeds, seizing opportunities, and learning new ways to blend is a delicate adventure with lifetime rewards. Fourteen exchange students and you would think my children were blendmasters. They are. Each of them in their own ways have learned to adapt and accept so easily. My children have had over a decade of accepting new faces, cultures, diversities, and families. I must remind myself that I was able to give them this incredible gift. This FES life was a privilege to all of us. Our lessons made us stronger advocates for acceptance. I can't expect others to share our way or be able to adapt as quickly as we can. Our way has been unusual and for many too unknown to try. Part of why I am writing this book of my experience is to help boost the courage needed to step out and try the hosting experience.

Sometimes recognizing the difference between adapting and adjusting is viewed differently. And sometimes people just don't want change. And sometimes, like this girl, others do see the issue and are trying their best to make change. This sweet girl acknowledged the struggle of investing. Questions like: How can she add another "mom" when her mom is amazing? Where do these "siblings" fit into her heart? She too had to be patient, waiting and searching for how it would all blend. Along with her, I had to be patient and just keep seizing moments.

Lucky for us all it turns out the patience paid off rather quickly. It was about halfway into the exchange the first time our grandson came over and asked for her by name.

When she heard him use her name, she was a bit emotional. That moment she became invested in him. Little kids aren't in her daily life, so the lane was wide open in her heart. After that, there was almost a domino effect. She found places for all of us. She started going out more with friends. She began to soften to the possibility of us connecting to her life. We just needed to be patient and wait for the moment to happen and for her to find the places where we fit into her already full life!

With every up there is a down. She went to the mall with friends. I was tempted to take pictures of the event because I was beyond excited. Such a seemingly small event was a big progressive adventure for her! Hours later I received a call from an upset parent. The group our FES went with ran into a scary situation. A man in the parking garage got angry with the group for parking too close and he pulled out a screwdriver and began to stab their car!!!! Culture shock, crazy shock. No one was injured and the girls now have a great story, but I finally got her to go somewhere without us and this is her first solo experience.

Thankfully, she jumped right back on the horse and went with friends again. She also went with our daughter to a sleepover. I adore when my FES go to different homes. We all do things differently so learning life outside our home is a vital part of the exchange. She even went to church with them! Again, religion can be a very delicate subject where FES are concerned. I talked about my own struggle with Mary vs. Martha and advocating going to church services falls into a tricky category. I want my FES to go to church while here. I want them to go to many churches while here! What is "usual Sunday Service" to us can be so educational, cultural, and life changing! For me,

I don't advocate church services based on religion. I base the attendance the same as any other cultural experience. Things as simple as song lyrics on a big screen or in house coffee shops can be game changers to a young person's view of "Church Folk"! I am no theologian but from my small research every religion wants to be heard, they want to share. Isn't that Kind Growth?

With all the newfound activities and friends, she was still true to herself. She still did everything that made her happy and settled. She loved to sit in the kitchen and drink her tea. She probably snuck a few too many snacks as well. She developed quite a cheez-it addiction! Gaining weight here in America is something all our FES have done. For a mixture of reasons like new flavors and presentations, ultimately portion control is hard to manage with our restaurant style helpings. She loved to nap and chill. By being patient, I got to really know this new daughter who was comfortable in her own company. She enjoys quiet time in her space.

There is such a peaceful place when you flip your perspectives. I had thought she was avoiding me and I was focused on her avoidance. When I switched my perspective to forging a way into her heart vs. waiting for her to open to me, I got the gift I pursued! Other FES taught me I don't have to be right. This FES brought clarity to the fact it isn't about me! It isn't cause and effect. Time to adjust those sails again. If I get too caught in the self-absorbed place, I lose moments. I rob myself of experiences because I am too caught up in how it affects me. This young woman was confident in herself. Her value. I could accept her as is or I could whine and make it about me. I am so glad she showed me the value of patience.

In the spring I surprised the girls with a quick trip to Florida for spring break. We took several days with time to just be. It's a balancing act of how much you play tour guide to your FES and how much you just "be". Her parents purchased a gorgeous meal for all of us as a returned thank you for this trip. Receiving appreciation is a learned skill. I am putting it in print as a reminder to myself! Thank You, my dear sweet Dutch family!

Later that spring, she also decided to join the track team. She really enjoyed her time involved with this team. It's never too late to make some new friends. She was learning how to make room for new people in her life at the same time I was learning how to accept a role I understood very differently now. Young adults are finding their way. They don't see how their actions or inactions can be hurtful. Babies are born selfish and greedy. Kids develop those same traits. As parents we need to guide them with boundaries and rules. Young adults also can have a "me" mentality. In my experience with FES, however, rules often have a negative reception and are viewed more as dictates. I couldn't dictate that she invests in me. Building bridges, planting seeds, and seizing opportunities are all teachable moments without dictates. Allowing teachable moments gives each side opportunities to grow. Having the patience to wait for the moment when all that work pays off is a skill I will keep applying to my life.

Another first, orthodontics! Wow, what an amazing group of dental workers right here. They helped us navigate her records being transferred, getting her invisalign set, managed her care, and surprise she went home with her retainers. All this managed within a pandemic. I have always gone to the same dental group, and I really have no intention of changing. However, taking my sweet Dutch girl to a dentist new to me reminded me of that small town mentality I have been kindly growing to absolve. I am so glad I got to meet this dental group. I could not have walked into that new dental office with the same curiosity had I not begun hosting all these years ago. Differences aren't scary to me anymore!

As a family we learned things about ourselves during each FES stay. Sometimes what we learned was downright ridiculous! With this FES, we learned we talked about poop almost every night at dinner.
What?!?!
Yep, I had no idea.
Our FES pointed it out one night after our youngest daughter had a very not so graceful belch!!!! Sure, enough over the next few weeks we observed the continuous poop talk. The baby filled his diaper one night, the dog farted another, we had a squeaky chair that sounded flatulent, and an occasional "that tastes like shit" comment. One night we had almost made the entire meal without a poop incident, when a friend stopped over and literally said "I gotta poop" as she scurried into the bathroom. It was a bonus, when my husband decided to shit himself (not really, but it smelled like it) in the Dollar General! Although that may be our FES's favorite memory of her time in America! Well, that, or when he ordered a "Corbin Ruben" from Starbucks!

It was also very interesting to learn how much we simply go out for dinner. I learned there is a very large difference between going out FOR dinner and going out TO dinner. We usually go out for dinner because we worked late or had appointments. We will load up, go grab a quick bite, and head home. We don't do much fast food, but we do eat out often. We learned when our FES goes out to dinner they often dress up, enjoy multiple small courses, and often spend hours chatting over coffee or drinks after dinner. What a different take on visiting a restaurant. We do get pretty caught up in the rat race, fast pace, got to get it done mentality. And let's not forget, servers making tip wages would probably have our heads if we occupied their sections for too long. Still, I know I am forever grateful that my FES taught me to slow down, to observe my actions, to make moments count, and not just count the moments!

She loved to shop - and it took her forever to make decisions! Just like going out to dinner, here we tend to rush shopping as well. She would decide on what boots she wanted and take several trips to the store before she ever actually purchased them! She had patience in so many things (I did not). It took her almost an hour one shopping trip to decide on a perfume purchase. On a different trip she identified a smell that her mom likes, and I was like - me to grab it for me let's go! Ironically, that scent is now my favorite and a daily reminder to be patient!

This girl was so quiet and reserved up until her last couple months. She had found places for so many new people in her heart, yet she still seemed to be holding back. A combination of new activities, medication change, and attitude made a transformation in her exchange year. Maybe a straighter smile contributed some too! People who tried to talk to her all year could now talk to her. She smiled more and was open to those around her. She welcomed conversations! What a change! At home she laughed more and made herself vulnerable having some great conversations with us all. She cooked a Dutch meal. All the amazing things that happen during an exchange happened in those final months. Sometimes resistance to change is cultural and sometimes it's just stubbornness. I think she had an equal mix.

The last days of her visit were so difficult. Wanting to add time, to just keep her a bit longer. I talked about fighting my way into her heart, but she was in mine now too! Others have made the observation of the rotating door of people living in our home. I don't see it that way. I wanted that door simply left open. I had to work hard to get those doors open figuratively and literally! The triumph that comes and the emotions I feel when a FES texts and says, "Can I facetime you, I miss your voice." Just before she left our Azerbaijan FES came to visit for his sister's graduation so these two FES got to meet which is always such an amazing reward to me! I wanted to add time. I wanted her to know the door was always open. My heart would always be open!

We had a large graduation/going away party for our youngest and for the FES. Many people came and brought extraordinary gifts. It was a beautiful time of love and joy shared in support of my family. Our FES was blown away by the number of people who stopped by. It doesn't matter where you live, if you allow others to be part of your journey you will win!

We did eventually make the second airport stop.

It sucked!

The following day our grandson asked for her by name. He was a pro at saying her name now, but it took me right back to the moment......... when he said her name to her the first time. It was then I realized her name from his lips was a game changer in her exchange year and now this would be my grandson's first time he was aware and would be letting go of a FES. Not even three years old and he would be learning kind growth!

I may have leaked a little sending her off the day before but there was no holding back the tears when a sweet little boy wanted his FES!

Apparently, moments have a twisted sense of humor because that moment I had years ago when I sent rookie FES home, that uncontrollable moment of tears I had fought so hard to overcome revisited me again. Nothing could stop it. The buckets of snot and tears and gut-wrenching hiccups, it all happened again!!!   The FES life went full circle, it all started with an amazing cry and now ended with a cry too!

Several months after she left, the same three-year-old grandson was in the kitchen applying way too many temporary train tattoos. For whatever three-year-old reason when he got to the caboose the only spot, he wanted it was on his butt!!! Logical, I suppose. I really missed my Netherlands girl at that moment. She would have been sitting there in the kitchen, sipping her tea, and most likely hysterically laughing over the butt tattoo! This is one more reminder to always appreciate those small things, because they are actually the big things if you allow them in your heart! Remember it takes patience to get to the .....moment!

After each and every FES took their second flight, I immediately cleaned out the rooms and prepared for our next adventure. I didn't do it this time; I still haven't done it. Her room has not been cleared out. Her left behind stuff is still here. Her pictures are still on the walls in her bedroom. We all still call it her room. Sure, I clean it from time to time, but for now it's just going to be "her room".

And I will wait until I see her again...because the FES life and family just keeps growing.

Lessons I Learned

Kind Growth x 14

1. Norway - Rookie FES! This one taught me how to be an international parent!
2. Azerbaijan - This FES taught me to use a telescope vs. a microscope. I also learned hate is a real thing.
3. Germany - This FES taught me that my reactions have value, however, I don't have to be right.
4. China - This FES taught me today is the day to learn something new.
5. Germany - this FES taught me to Relax! There are lots of options inside the gray palette of life!!!!
6. Venezuela - This FES taught me to love people where they are.
7. Norway - This FES taught me that if I chase storms I will get rained on, and I will find a rainbow in the process.
8. Germany - This FES taught me to value my journey.
9. Republic Of Georgia - This FES taught me that Patriotism is powerful and can be crippling without acceptance of others.
10. Italy - Baby FES! This one taught me I am worth it!
11. Brazil - This FES taught me to remember to live in each moment.
12. Taiwan - This FES taught me that filters are good for coffee not people.
13. Spain - This FES taught me to see the colors.
14. Netherlands - This FES taught me the power that comes - patiently waiting for the moment!

Epilogue
My Words:

Fourteen exchange kids.
Four biological kids.
Eighteen teenagers and friends that rotated through one home.
Digest that - 18 teenagers in one home and we didn't even have a reality show! So many religions, cultures, races, sexualities, and palettes of diversity. We had heated discussions, differences for sure, but acceptance from all!!!
When you're willing to grow the details organically change.
I now challenge all my readers through this book to accept differences and be willing to change your thought process.
My first step to acceptance was changing my thought process.

There are so many words in our language that speak to divide and hate. If you try every day to take one word that has negative publicity surrounding it and redefine it positively you will succeed in kind growth! It's like climbing a staircase, don't let the destination scare you - just take that first step, find your balance, then take another step.

Progress is:
P: Positive
R: Rate
O: of
G: Growth
R: Remembering
E: Everyone's
S: Someone
S: Special

My amazing group of international children and their families have taught me to love everything inside me and allow it to complement everything outside me.

If you want to see change in the world - Be the Kind Growth - you want to see!

FES Words:

When I reached out to others along my journey of writing, people mentioned that it would be interesting to hear the personal perspectives from the FES themselves.

What did they learn?
What kind growth did the FES have?

They were right. I had focused all my attention on my growth and advocating for acceptance while I made this venture to write a book. I accepted the challenge of asking them to share their kind growth.

I discovered it was a horrible and brilliant challenge as I received the responses:

1) It was a horrible challenge because as the FES responded I realized I did affect them!
2) It was a brilliant challenge because I realized I did affect them!

Here are a few of the responses for you to enjoy for yourselves!

Italy Baby FES:

In the time I was there i learnt not to just hear but to listen to people, it started as a way to learn English and the culture but then became a way to get to know people in a deeper way. I'm forever grateful to the family that's hosted me because it tought me the best lessons there is to know (imo) "different is just different not worst" I'm bringing this motto with me wherever I go and it is making me a happier person

Brazil FES:

I didn't think it was possible to feel part of a family without being the one I was born in, but being an exchange student made me learn that yes, this is possible and I will always have a huge affection for them. (About you)

One thing I have noticed is that Americans are extremely competitive, they always need to be the best/first, sometimes they need to slow down a little and enjoy being average. (About the society)

Azerbaijan FES:

So, as 17 year kid, kid from Azerbaijan came to US. life is so different, mindset is different. at the beginning it was hard, different everything including food, lifestyle.

what I learned?! I was 17 yr old kid, I learned before u made choices u have to think, think and then act. if u will win,u r winner. if u will lose, dont get upset. learn from it and move forward. bcs it was ur choice and now u have to deal with it.
the main important thing i learned different is different not wrong.

Norway Rookie FES parents:

Our son living with you has been a gift.
a)   We didn't fully understand how much being a FES with his American family influenced our son until he came back home and wasn`t just a year older. In conversation we quickly understood he matured socially
b)   Through our FES son we also made new friends. It isn`t just the student who benefits. Our horizon and family was also broadened culturally.

Norway Rookie FES sister:

When my brother said he was spending a year in the U.S, I was 15 years old and ready to experience the life of an only child. In my precocious mind I remember thinking a year abroad would do him good. Surely he would mature from being a foreigner and teenager in a town so small that one would miss it if blinking when driving through.

It's been 13 years since he boarded a plane to the Midwest, where he got to know the family that would enrich us all with long-standing transatlantic friendships. These special people shared their home, values, humour and opinions with my brother, and in the years that followed, the rest of his family too. In ways it felt like we were all foreign exchange students: learning and growing from my brother's experiences across the pond.

I am grateful for the endless conversations through the years on everything from presidential elections, Walmart dress-code, and Amish beard-cutting cases. Thank you for opening your home to my brother, and for extending the generosity to the rest of us. What an example of the things that can happen when one decides to meet what´s foreign with an open mind.

Netherlands FES:

During my exchange I have gained a lot of life experience. The reason I decided to go on exchange to the USA was to take some time to experience more and learn about traveling alone and living with a different family. It was so much harder and different than I imagined. There were many cultural differences mostly in the small things like going out to eat and how people dress. I had to learn to adjust to a completely different 'normal' life. It was very interesting and hard at some points but my host family has been amazing at making me feel at home. I am an only child and I have always wanted siblings. This exchange gave me the opportunity to live in a big family. Words can't equal how thankful I am for hosting me. I grew as a person and my exchange helped me to get more out of my comfort zone and being independent. I will never forget all the memories I made during my year of exchange.

But I think most important of the whole experience is that I can call the family who hosted me a second family and I can't wait to see everyone again.

Netherlands FES Parents:

It has been an extraordinary and amazing year for our daughter and for us as parents, our only child of 17-18 years, going overseas to the family in Ohio, 10 months for a high school exchange during Covid-19 period. From the first acquaintance with our daughters host mom we trusted our child to their care for 100%. Our daughter as a young girl learned to experience and to adjust to a complete different culture. The struggle in the beginning, also because of Corona restrictions, has been difficult. But after some months she adjusted and felt happy although she always stayed connected with her own values and personal and cultural characteristics. She mostly learned to make new friends, to be more open and social with people (from another culture) and to have a more wider perspective of the world. The hospitality of the host family and her always caring FES mother, her cool sister, and chill FES father has given her an experience she will never forget and gave her an extra family forever.

Italy FES's parents:

You are never ready for your children to leave. But when the reason is a study-life experience abroad, you overcome any obstacle because what they"ll receive in return has no comparison with any other experience. Personally, we were very satisfied. Also, knowing that the host family had already had other experiences with "guests" encouraged us. And, I'd say, with good reason! In fact, he still keeps in touch with them nowadays and we can only be happy about it. Thanks Host family!
We haven't had such a long-lasting hospitality experience. However, we have been able to confirm what we've always affirmed: the exchange of ideas, habits, traditions, can only make you "grow".

Everyone should have this chance.

China FES:

I've only lived with this family for a short while. It was sometime around Christmas when I was picked up and told that they had to place me with a different family. I remember the ride. It was cold and dark and I was scared. But then I got to her house, it was warm and smelled like cookies. This new family was probably the nicest and funniest people I've ever met my entire life.

It's funny when my host mom asked me if I wanted to write something for her book, I badly wanted to but I just couldn't seem to remember wat exactly happened that winter ten years ago. Memories might fade but feelings won't. I would never forget how she and her family welcomes me into their home and treated me as one of their own. For a sixteen year old girl who was alone in a country thousands of miles away from home and being tole that she needed to move out and wait for someone to take her in was kind of a scary situation to be in. But then she was there. She gave me the strength to be brave. I'm eternally grateful for the kindness's and love she and her family showed me when I needed them most. Looking back now, all I could remember was how happy I was when I lived with them and how much I wished I never had to leave.

I remember eaing raw cookie dough- it was awful!

I remember going to basketball games.

I was so lucky to have met her and have her in my life my dearest. I couldn't imagine what life would have turned out without you. Thank you for bringing so much light into my life and helped me become who I am today. Love you to the moon and back xxx

Taiwan FES:

As a Taiwanese, studying has been the main purpose in my past twenty years. (except the year as a foreign exchange student:)) Most of my childhood memories was going to cram schools, and I didn't get a lot of chances to explore my interests. The boarding high school I went to in Taiwan even had "fake" clubs, which we usually called "club classes". We couldn't actually choose which club we wanted to join and teachers were able to give lectures or tests during that period of time. This kind of education system made me completely lost when I had to choose a major for college because I had no clue which field I'm

interested in. I was so scared and flustered, and that was one of the reasons why I decided to be a foreign exchange student in my senior year of high school. I wanted to find "myself".

However, being a foreign exchange student wasn't as easy as I thought. The first challenge I encountered was the language part, which I never thought it would be such a big deal. I have been learning English as my foreign language since I was in kindergarten. While other kids were playing in the playground, I went to English classes after school. When I arrived in the US, I found out that I understand most part of others' conversations. But the problem was I had nearly no ability to express my thoughts, I didn't know "when" to say the right thing. Especially when there's a group of people having conversations, I had to rethink my words in order to let it out. It turned out that most of the time when I was ready to speak, the conversation was already over. My confidence about my English skills suddenly collapsed. I started to talk less and be quiet.

After the exchange year and being back in Taiwanese education, I discovered why I would act like that. All of our tests and exams usually have only ONE correct answer. (most of them are multiple choice questions) Specially, our English learning system was lack of speaking and writing courses. Along with being used to answering test questions, I personally lost the ability to have my own thoughts and the capacity of describing my perceptions. Now in retrospect, I wish I had the courage to make more mistakes and I wish I could have speak more.

"Different is different, not wrong." I still bring this quote with me nowadays, and I will keep keeping it aside me in the future. In Chinese culture, children are trained to be as same as others. A notable example is that we have to wear uniforms until we graduated from high school. As we growing up, we are afraid of being "different". We're scared of having different opinions from others. We're scared to act different from others. We want to be the same as other people. For example, my classmates and friends all went to cram schools, and that made me felt like I NEED to, too. Just because the people around me did so. Nevertheless, during my exchange year, I found out that it's not odd at all for Americans to talk about their own differences, and that made me doubted myself. If I'm afraid of being different, how am I going to find my true self? I started to face my differences. I stopped going to cram schools and tutoring. I started to find my real needs, which was studying alone in my bedroom.

After a year of exchange, I came back to Taiwan and faced the college entrance exam. This time, I did not hesitate to choose Applied Linguistic and Language Study as my major. My Chinese teacher tried to talk me out of it, since she knew how hard it would be as a language learner in Taiwan. (Working opportunity is not as manifold as others.) But I know there's no right or wrong answer. It's just different. I also started baking in my free times. I'm really glad that I actually found what I'm interested in and

I'm so grateful to have the chance of being a foreign exchange student.

All of these responses from my international family and friends emotionally touched my heart. To know so many of them still carry my spoken words with them.....

"Different is Different NOT Wrong" is such a comfort.

I found my kind growth!
They all found their kind growth!
Now it's your turn to go find your KIND GROWTH!

Surprise Words:

My youngest daughter surprised me with this next edition:
She asked her siblings about their growth.
Here are their responses from growing up FES?

My oldest boy:

Different is different not wrong.

My oldest daughter:

It was an interesting many of years that impacted our
family. Looking back, I never formed a close bond with any
of the FES, regardless it is something that played a big part
in my life. There were so many memories we made, and
experiences we had together. Each one brought
something new to the table.
 Plus, the vacation destinations are a bonus-Norway was a
blast.

My youngest son:

Having exchange students open my eyes to how I wanted to live life. I had exchange students that came from money, some middle class like me, and some who thought flushing toilets inside was a novelty. I have learned how to deal with people who don't share the same values and traditions as me, but I have also learned how to embrace the traditions and values of others.   I have learned to be taught and to teach other traditions: all while accepting our differences. I learned different is different NOT wrong!

What that means to me is in life, you will always meet someone with different ways of doing life. Differences from their religion, speech, and morals but they are still people just like me.

The more I learned about other cultures the more I learned about myself and how I wanted my life to be.
My Norway Brothers taught me to enjoy my environment. From my Germany brothers I learned how to stand up for myself even when everyone disagreed with me. From my Azerbaijan I learned to value the things I have and never stop learning.
Living life to the fullest and embracing everyone as family! That's what my Venezuelan brother taught me.

My Italian taught me what family was all about!

From Brazil I learned it was ok to be different and find fun in learning the things I don't understand.

Taiwan showed me how words can make living here a real mean place.

I learned I have to truly embrace a culture before I can understand it from Netherlands.

My brother from Georgia taught me, some people just don't want to blend, doesn't mean you can't all get along. You can be best friends and they will still like what they like and you what you like.

All of my exchange siblings left a mark on me that made me who I am and for that I love them all!

I have gone to see some of them – I want to go see them all. They are my family. Venezuela died a coupe years ago, at the time he died I hadn't seen him for about 2 years. I had talked to him every week – he was one of my closest brothers. I didn't see the impact he had on me until I lost him. I cried for hours, thinking of him and all the memories we made together, the all night heart to heart talks we would have, and all the life lessons he taught me. These FES, my family are real family to me.

I lost a brother!

Exchange student will change your mindset, your morals, your patience, but most importantly it will change your heart.

My love for my biological family grew because of my exchange family.

Family to me isn't just mom, dad, siblings.......

It's people around you that care about you, help you, and put you in check when your out of line.

So, for me family is mom, dad, 12 brothers and 5 sisters.

Shout out to my mom for writing this book.   She is such a strong, beautiful, and mindful person.   I hope this book not only shows you that having an exchange student comes with good and bad experiences.   I hope it shows you the love and potential your family can gain by having one.

FE improved my life, and I couldn't thank them or my parents enough for letting me grow up FES life!   Truly THANK YOU!

...

My youngest daughter:

For most of the FES they say that the one year they spent with my family is something they will cherish forever, an extraordinary year. For me, it has been an extraordinary life.

Ever since I was around 5 ½ years old, I have been welcoming and saying goodbye to so many family members. Hard to accept at first, but I learned. I also had to learn to share EVERY aspect of my life. Which did not come easily the more I grew up, but I still did my best to be a good sister.

Being so young to start out I do not remember many specific details about early FES, just that they made a lasting impression through kindness on a young girl. As I grew, my relationships with the FES in my life were able to grow stronger. I am glad that I am able to keep in touch with many of the FES today.

Having 14 extra siblings, plus some extra parents, (I adopted my Norwegian parents) provided me with a lifetime of memories that I will cherish forever. So much frustration, laughter, tears, love, friendships-more like family, and bowel movements (some VERY bad...Azerbaijan). One even pointed out how much us Americans talk about our movements, at the dinner table none the less (Netherlands).

Overall, I would not change anything about any of my biological or FES families. Each person has their own story that impacted me in some way or another, and in the end its about accepting that different is different and not wrong.

Thoughts About Words:

Some words I really had to evaluate in my FES LIFE-
These began as words I journaled because I questioned
them.

Words I looked up definitions to. The words I struggled to
apply easily in my life.

Then words that evolved as I was able to connect personal
experiences to them.
The definitions to me changed, and that journal became
this book.

Now these words have meaning to me, and I can apply
them to my life from personal experiences.

When you see these words in the book know the following
definitions are what come from my heart to the page.

Religion: In all forms is sacred, respect it, love it. Accept
your way is perfect for you - not so much for someone else.
If your goal is for someone to join your beliefs, then set
about living the life you want them to see. Plant the seeds,
seize the moments, and you do the work. The power of
accountability is yours!

Racism: Do I see color - heck yes, I do - and I love learning
the cultures and characters beneath every shade! Identify
individuals because they are awesome, and you want to
learn about them.

Culture: Is an umbrella term - it covers a lot. To truly learn a single person's culture, you need to get rained on. Many cultural things are a habit, to understand YOU personally - have to show the growth and not the person you're learning about.

Bigotry: Being way too attached to an opinion isn't attractive - clear the filters.

Hypocrite: Relax or you will be! Learn that gray is as much a color as black and white.

Hate: It's ok to be scared. Value the journey of your life but don't hate someone else's path!

Black lives matter, white lives matter, blue lives matter, all lives matter. How can we possibly put more value on any life past, present, or future, than another life? If you want something to focus on, try learning about each other. We each have a story that has nothing to do and everything to do with culture, color, religion, position, or finance. Life matters, so live one that leaves a kind growth legacy!

Diversity: How many times do I have to say it? Different is Different, NOT Wrong! Accept people where they are! Identifying differences for the means of equality is a kindness we all need to demonstrate.

Fixed mindset to Growth mindset: A fixed immovable heart isn't going to change - so grow that heart a bit! If you're not sure how to start, watch the Grinch!

White privilege: Is an inheritance. I doubt anyone would be ashamed of a monetary inheritance. Take stands of positivity.

Patriotism: Is a love of home.

Final Words:

It takes the largest amount of courage to be kind and the smallest amount of wisdom for growth.

I am thirty-three years old (that's what I have been telling everyone anyway)
I believe opened at home, is the same as homemade
I have been fat
I have been lazy
I have learned growth
I have been kind
I have had my vision checked
I have been patient
I am excited when I look in the mirror and see a person willing to love because I learned how to see people and definitely not because I accepted the status quo!

I hope everyone of my FES KNOW that I am forever a better person for knowing them!   Each of them changed me in ways I can never thank them for.

I will always advocate for acceptance for them and for me.

To my own biological children, I surrounded you all with endless love and possibilities so please take me along with you on your next adventures. I am handing over the reins.

To my husband, we did it! We fought the battles that needed fighting, learned to listen, and practiced patience.

Made in the USA
Monee, IL
26 April 2022